AMERICAN PROTESTANTISM

American

THE CHICAGO HISTORY OF AMERICAN CIVILIZATION

Daniel J. Boorstin, EDITOR

Protestantism

By Winthrop S. Hudson

 THE UNIVERSITY OF CHICAGO PRESS

CHICAGO AND LONDON

To

My daughters

Judith *and* Susan

The University of Chicago Press, Chicago and London
The University of Toronto Press, Toronto 5, Canada

© *1961 by The University of Chicago. Published 1961*
Fourth Impression 1966
Printed in the United States of America

Editor's Preface

With remarkable cogency, Mr. Hudson here describes what has been distinctively American about Protestantism in America. This he does not by cataloguing the diversity of Protestant groups, but by discovering the kind of unity that has persisted and how the diversity itself has expressed our culture as a whole. He has drawn on vast, miscellaneous, and scattered sources; the conciseness and coherence of his conclusions are impressive.

One of the puzzling facts about our history is how American Protestantism has maintained any identifiable unity. This unity, as Mr. Hudson sees it, has come not only from a long common tradition but also from the simple fact that Protestantism has been the majority religion—a residual religion—in a nation held together by elusive majorities.

Protestantism, according to Mr. Hudson, has had to pay a price for its predominance. If we accept his interpretation, Protestantism has been more transformed by its American experience than has either Catholicism or Judaism. The tendencies bred by its majority status help explain its difficulties in the twentieth century. From being the predominant religion of American culture, American Protestantism has tended to become a culture-religion—more concerned to adjust itself to the culture than vice versa. This volume tells us how the assimilation took place during the nineteenth century, and how it has threatened to put a religion of Americanism in place of American religions.

Mr. Hudson is impressed not only by the peculiar perils to Protestantism in America but also by the fertility, multiformity, and versatility of the Protestant tradition here. He is especially successful in describing the American phenomenon of "denominationalism" under which different Protestant groups claim no monopoly on the Christian word, but only a right to compete for adherents within an ecumenical Protestant community. He notes the decisive importance of the westward movements for American evangelicalism, of the quickly growing city for the rise of new institutions like the Y.M.C.A. and for the competition of non-Protestant groups, of the fluid suburbs for the rise of the community church, and of a host of other facts of American social history for the special character of American Protestantism.

The changes through which American Protestantism has passed, as Mr. Hudson outlines them, raise profound questions about the direction of American civilization. An "American Protestantism," he says, had taken shape by about 1787. During the next century and a quarter, America was shaped in an essentially Protestant mold; it was the era of a "Protestant America." After 1914, he sees a "Post-Protestant America," when the accumulating forces of the earlier period—immigra-

tion, evangelicalism, "theological erosion," rural concentration—combined with those of a newer era to put Protestantism
on the defensive. Protestantism began to lose the prerogatives,
and also some of the temptations, of a majority religion. In
this new test, Mr. Hudson observes, may be the opportunity
for Protestantism not merely to express America, as it did in
the nineteenth century, but even to challenge America.

The "Chicago History of American Civilization" aims to
make each aspect of our culture a window to all our history.
The series contains two kinds of books: a *chronological* group,
which provides a coherent narrative of American history from
its beginning to the present day; and a *topical* group, which
deals with the history of varied and significant aspects of
American life. This book is one of the topical group. It com-
plements two other volumes in the series: John Tracy Ellis,
American Catholicism, and Nathan Glazer, *American Judaism.*

DANIEL J. BOORSTIN

Table of Contents

Table of Contents

I

The Shaping of American
Protestantism, 1607-1787

The very title of this book provokes a question. How can one speak of American Protestantism? At first sight, American Protestantism appears so varied and multiform as to preclude any attempt to deal with it as a single historical entity. Institutionally, American Protestantism is not one but many. It has no central organization. It has no officially adopted creed. It is bound together by no universally accepted liturgical forms. The structures of discipline and government are diverse. There is no great leader in its past around whom its loyalties may cluster, nor any golden age to which it can look with nostalgia as a norm. Instead of a single history, American Protestantism seems to have only a series of histories—the histories of individual denominations.

American Protestantism, on the other hand, has never been quite so diverse as a bare listing of Protestant groups would suggest. While there may be more than two hundred different Protestant bodies in the United States, most of them are small, almost minute in membership. Few have as many as fifty thousand adherents, and not more than eighteen can claim as many as five hundred thousand members. But these larger bodies and most of the smaller ones are grouped together in not more than six major denominational families. The complexity is still further reduced by the regional distribution of the Protestant denominations. Broadly speaking, there are no Presbyterians in New England and no Congregationalists in Pennsylvania; no Lutherans in Mississippi, no Episcopalians in the Dakotas, and no Disciples or "Christians" in New Jersey. Thus in most communities, there are few Protestants who are not included within the membership of six or seven different churches.

Although the situation is much less complex than the statistics seem to indicate, it would still be difficult to speak of American Protestantism were it not for the fact that most of the Protestant churches—in spite of their institutional differences—have been shaped to a common pattern. European visitors to the United States have usually been much more impressed by the similarities among American Protestants than by their differences. In the same way, American delegates to ecumenical assemblies have frequently found that they stood nearer to one another than any of them did to the respective bodies to which they were related by parentage and tradition. This common pattern is not of recent origin but a legacy from colonial America.

The clue to an understanding of American Protestantism can be found in Edmund Burke's celebrated *On Conciliation with the American Colonies*, a speech which he delivered on the eve of the American Revolution (March 22, 1775). He was seeking to help his fellow members of Parliament understand the "love of freedom" and "fierce spirit of liberty" that was so powerful a motivation among the American colonists. "The people of the colonies," he reminded them, "are descendants of Englishmen."

England, Sir, is a nation which still I hope respects, and formerly adored, her freedom. The colonists emigrated from you when this part of your character was most predominant; and they took this bias and direction the moment they parted from your hands. They are therefore not only devoted to liberty, but to liberty according to English ideals, and on English principles.

Furthermore, Burke continued, "the people are Protestants; and of that kind which is the most adverse to all implicit subjection of mind and opinion. This is a persuasion not only favorable to liberty, but built upon it." English and Protestant. These are two key words to describe the American colonies, and they serve to explain not only the colonists' "fierce spirit of liberty" but also to a large degree both the diversity and the unity of American Protestantism. The diversity was largely a British importation which was fostered and protected first by English and then by British colonial policy. The unity was partly the product of the formative influence exerted by the American environment, but essentially it was the product of a specific Protestant tradition which Burke identified as the dominant theological inheritance from abroad.

Not all the colonists, to be sure, were of English descent, but seven out of ten of the white population were of English blood and almost nine out of ten were British. It was from England that the colonists derived their language, their political ideals and institutions, and their predominant culture. While non-English elements in the population made energizing contributions to the common life of the colonies, assimilation into the

English stock and conformity to the English mode of life was the general pattern. Even those of non-English descent gradually became accustomed to speaking of their "rights as Englishmen." Nor were all the colonists Protestants. Most did not belong to any church. But of those who were connected in one way or another with a church, the overwhelming majority were Protestants. Indeed, they were almost exclusively Protestants. While membership statistics are lacking, the relative strength is shown by the number of congregations of each group. The most reliable enumeration of colonial congregations gives these figures for 1775: Congregational, 668; Presbyterian, 588; Anglican, 495; Baptist, 494; Quaker, 310; German Reformed, 159; Lutheran, 150; Dutch Reformed, 120; Methodist, 65; Roman Catholic, 56; Moravian, 31; Congregational-Separatist, 27; Dunker, 24; Mennonite, 16; French Reformed, 7; Sandemanian, 6; Jewish, 5; Rogerene, 3. The distribution of congregations was 98.4 per cent Protestant, 1.4 per cent Roman Catholic, and three-twentieths of 1 per cent Jewish. These statistics bear eloquent testimony to the fact that the overwhelming majority of the colonists were Protestant in affiliation or background and also to the fragmentation of American Protestantism into many independent bodies. Since the need for religious uniformity within a civil state had been regarded as axiomatic for more than ten centuries in western Christendon, the diversity of American Protestantism requires some explanation.

· 1 ·

PROTESTANT DIVERSITY

The American colonies were English colonies, and the multiplicity of Protestant bodies in colonial America was largely the product of a policy of toleration pursued by the authorities at home with regard to the new settlements. Initially, to be sure, it was assumed that there would be and should be uniformity of religion in his majesty's dominions beyond the seas. The instructions of James I in the first charter of Virginia were that "the true word and service of God" should be "preached, planted, and used" in the new colony "according to the doctrine, rites, and religion now professed and established within our realm of England," and from the beginning there were laws to enforce conformity. The significant fact, however, was that these laws were seldom rigorously enforced. The second Virginia charter of 1609, for example, contained the specific provision that "none be permitted to pass in any voyage . . . to be made into said country but such as first shall have taken the Oath of Supremacy," and yet the Separatists from Leyden who landed at Plymouth in 1620 had set sail with permission from the Virginia Company to establish a settlement within its territory. Equally significant is the fact that in no colony other than Virginia did the English authorities even attempt to impose a pattern of religious uniformity.

Enriching a trading nation.—One of the important factors determining English religious policy in the colonies was the fact that the colonies were commercial ventures designed to contribute to the prosperity of a developing empire. To be profitable the colonies had to have settlers to clear the forests and till the fields. It was not always easy to persuade people to leave their homes and run the risks of life in a new land. The jails could be and were emptied to provide colonists. The impoverished were sent out on condition that the passage money be repaid by a term of indentured servitude. Such people had little to lose and much to gain in forsaking their homes and beginning life anew in a distant wilderness. It was obvious, however, that a sturdier type of settler could be recruited among members of oppressed religious sects, to whom the prospect of toleration provided a powerful incentive to accept the hazards of life in the American colonies. William Penn recruited settlers from among the minority groups of the Rhineland, and his desire to furnish refuge for his fellow Quakers added a personal inducement to attempt to establish a policy of toleration in his colony. In much the same way, Lord Baltimore sought to attract settlers to Maryland with a promise of toleration, hoping that it would permit his fellow Roman Catholics to be tolerated. A similar policy was adopted in New Jersey and Delaware, and liberty of conscience for Protestant Christians was specifically guaranteed in the charters of the Carolinas and Georgia. In New York the Articles of Capitulation of 1664 provided that the Dutch inhabitants be given freedom of worship, and the instructions of James II to the governor in 1682 directed him to "permit all persons of what religion soever quietly to inhabit" and not to give them "any disturbance or disquiet whatsoever for or by reason of their differing opinions in matters of religion."

The economic advantage of such a policy was made explicit in the instructions which were sent to Peter Stuyvesant in New Amsterdam. The charter of New Netherlands had stated that "no other religion shall be publicly admitted in New Netherlands except the Reformed, as it is at present preached and practiced by public authority in the United Netherlands." Stuyvesant had attempted to carry out this provision by adopting rigorous measures to suppress dissent, but this led to his rebuke by the authorities at home. "Although it is our cordial desire that similar and other sectarians might not be found there," they wrote to him, "yet, as the contrary seems to be the fact, we doubt very much if vigorous proceedings against them ought not be discontinued, except you intend to check and destroy your population." The prosperity of old Amsterdam, he was reminded, was due in no small measure to the moderation of the magistrates in dealing with religious dissent, with the consequence that "people have flocked" from every land "to this asylum"; and he was informed that a similar policy should be pursued in New Amsterdam. "It is our opinion that some connivance would be useful; that the consciences of men, at least, ought ever to remain free and unshackled." A similar concern was expressed by the Lords of Trade in London in the instructions they sent to the Council of Virginia: "A free exercise of religion . . . is essential to enriching and improving a trading nation; it should be ever held sacred in His Majesty's colonies. We must, therefore, recommend it to your care that nothing be done which can in the least affect that great point." Edward Seymour had put it more bluntly a half-century earlier. An appeal had been made to London for the establishment of a college in Virginia, such as Massachusetts had in Harvard, for the training of ministers. An effort was made to enlist Seymour's help, and he was reminded that Virginians as well as New Englanders had souls to be saved. "Souls!" exclaimed Seymour, "Damn your souls. Make tobacco."

The influence of English domestic policy.—While considerations of economic advantage played their part in allowing religious diversity to develop, this factor alone is not sufficient to account for the relative equanimity with which dissent was viewed by both the English and the Dutch. It does not explain the radically different policies pursued in the French and Spanish colonies. The pressure of profit was no less strong in the French and Spanish colonies, but it was successfully resisted.

7

The significant difference seems to be that the "maxim of moderation" was already being practiced by the magistrates of old Amsterdam, while England was making halting progress in the same direction. In many ways, England did little more than export her own religious diversity.

Elizabeth, to be sure, had been completely emotional in her insistence upon outward conformity, but even Elizabeth had never wished "to make windows into men's hearts." While she was careful to prevent any widespread organization of dissent from developing and reacted vigorously to any invasion of what she considered to be her royal prerogative in matters religious, a great deal of latitude and practical freedom was permitted within the parishes. Nor did James I, despite his strong language, ever pursue a consistent and rigorous policy aimed at enforcing religious conformity. As a consequence, the stringent measures initiated by Archbishop Laud in the 1630's were regarded by many as intolerable innovations which justified the parliamentary revolt of the 1640's. With the meeting of the Long Parliament in 1640 all effective ecclesiastical control broke down. The victorious forces in the Civil War that followed were united in defense of "the good old cause," which was defined as a toleration that would include all save prelatists and papists. The latter were excluded largely for reasons of state rather than for religion. (The prelatists were exponents of the views of Archbishop Laud, whose intolerant policies had precipitated the Civil War, and thus they were regarded as a subversive element. The papists were regarded as a danger to the state because they were suspected of plotting to overthrow the government with the aid of French arms.) The restoration of the Stuarts in 1660 was followed in turn by the Glorious Revolution of 1688 and the accompanying Act of Toleration of 1689.

Since the toleration granted by this Act was limited to trinitarian Protestants, and thus excluded Unitarians, Jews, and Roman Catholics, it had the curious effect of restricting rather than extending toleration in some of the colonies. But in England and the other colonies the reverse was true. The significant fact is that for almost two-thirds of the whole colonial period a rather extensive toleration was the official policy of the English government at home as well as in the colonies.

The Dutch attitude toward dissent, of course, had been tempered by the struggle for Dutch Independence, but it was not unrelated to Calvin's admission in the Preface to the *Institutes* that it is impossible to draw precise boundaries to the Church of Christ, that is, it is not possible to determine with precision who is to be numbered among the faithful. It also was related to the parallel admission that "the purest churches under heaven are subject to mixture and error," and that consequently even the wisest and holiest of men and even the most representative of synods can make no claim to infallibility.

The English had an even more difficult time than their confreres abroad in insisting with good conscience upon the necessity for conformity among Protestants. The disputed points in England were largely related to the outward government of the church, and Archbishop Whitgift had acknowledged that "there is no one certain kind of government in the church which of necessity must be perpetually observed." In such matters— all the early Anglican apologists had insisted—it is left to the Christian prince to determine what is most suitable and convenient within his realm. It was on this basis that churches in other lands possessing an essentially evangelical faith—such as the Lutheran churches in Germany and Scandinavia and the Reformed churches in Switzerland, Holland, and Scotland—

were recognized as true churches. To the extent that it was difficult for the English authorities to insist upon conformity at home to that which was "nowhere in the Scripture prescribed," it was easy to tolerate dissent in the colonies; doubly so, when many of the dissenting churches—Scottish, Dutch, French, and German—were regarded as true churches when located in their respective homelands.

The New England story.—New England was the only area in colonial America in which a serious attempt was made to enforce religious uniformity, and in New England this attempt was made in spite of rather than because of English policy. The pattern was set by Massachusetts Bay, where the early settlers, having left their homes to establish a new Zion in the American wilderness, were determined to erect a "due form of government both civil and ecclesiastical" that would permit no dissent. The opportunity to do so arose out of the curious omission from the charter of the customary clause requiring the headquarters of the company to be in England and thus subject to the authority of the crown. As a consequence of this omission, the Massachusetts Bay Company was in effect an independent republic, for all the members of the company migrated to New England and took the charter with them. When the authorities at home finally discovered what had occurred, efforts were made to have the charter returned. The New Englanders, however, adopted the Fabian tactic of delay—making excuses, misunderstanding the communications they received, and finally ignoring the repeated requests for the charter. They knew that as long as they were able to keep the document on their side of the Atlantic their freedom of action was assured. The tactic of delay, of course, was made possible by the lapse of time which the long sea voyage necessitated in the interchange of communications, and it was further abetted by the Scottish invasion of England in 1639 which turned the attention of the English authorities to more pressing matters at home.

The attempt to suppress dissent in New England was never wholly successful. This was partly due to the fact that there was within the heart of New England Puritanism a never completely suppressed acknowledgment that "the Lord hath more truth yet to break forth out of his Holy Word" and that therefore they should be ever ready "to receive whatever truth shall be made known . . . from the written word of God." These are the words of John Robinson, but they were echoed in the writings of other New England divines. It was for this reason that New England Puritanism was always spawning its own dissidents—dissidents who appealed to the truth that had been made known to them from "the written word of God."

An equally important reason why the attempt to suppress dissent was never wholly successful in New England was that there was space enough for everyone. When the authorities of Massachusetts Bay were being condemned by their fellow Independents at home for their intolerance in banishing Roger Williams from the colony, John Cotton blandly suggested that no real injury had been done. His point was this:

> The jurisdiction (whence a man is banished) is but small, and the country round about it large and fruitful: where a man may make his choice of variety of more pleasant and profitable seats than he leaveth behind him. In which respect, banishment in this country is not counted as much a confinement as an enlargement.

The Massachusetts Bay authorities, to be sure, were not always content with mere banishment, but when they did attempt more explicit forms of coercion the open spaces of an empty land, to which Cotton had referred, tended to make them ineffective.

Dissenters did not need to go underground; they could just move. And move they did—across the river, through the woods, and over the mountains. From the sanctuary provided by open space and untilled acres, the contagion of dissent filtered back to the older settlements, making even more difficult the effort to compel conformity. Equally important was the spirit generated by vast stretches of empty land. A person who could always escape from the company of his fellows, if and when he wished, was not one who was apt to be unduly submissive. He thought of himself as a free man, with a mind of his own, independent of outward restraint. Such a person was not easily reduced to conformity.

Rhode Island represented the first great breach in the New England pattern of conformity established by Massachusetts Bay, but from a very early date Massachusetts Bay found it necessary, as Nathaniel Ward acknowledged, to "connive in some cases" with dissent. For some fifty years, however, Massachusetts Bay was able to pursue its independent course. The end of the attempt to enforce conformity was foreshadowed by the loss of the charter in 1684, and it was dramatically signalized in 1687 by the governor's seizure of the Old South meetinghouse for Anglican worship. Thereafter, although there was to be continuing trouble over taxes, the New Englanders had to conform to English policy; and not only the Anglicans but even Baptists and Quakers could worship freely according to the dictates of their own conscience.

Theological foundations of freedom.—If Protestant diversity in the American colonies was the product of the policy of religious toleration pursued by the English authorities, the diversity in turn ultimately created a situation in which there was no alternative to granting full religious freedom. The striking feature of this final consequence, however, was the fact that, for the most part, religious freedom was not thrust upon unwilling churches who accepted it merely as a practical necessity. Most of the churches by the end of the colonial period were ready both to welcome and to defend the principle of religious freedom on theological grounds.

This is a difficult point for many people to understand. Nathaniel Ward of Ipswich, a century earlier, had found it puzzling, for he believed that a person who "is willing to tolerate any religion . . . either doubts of his own, or is not sincere in it." Furthermore, it seemed clear to him that anyone who "is willing to tolerate any unsound opinion that his own may be tolerated, though never so sound, will for a need hang God's Bible at the Devil's girdle."

There is much to be said for Ward's point of view. People are tolerant in those areas in which they have no strong convictions. And religious indifference did contribute to the achievement of religious freedom in America. Benjamin Franklin supported the cause of religious liberty, we may suppose, largely for this reason. A few weeks before his death, Franklin responded to an inquiry by President Stiles of Yale concerning his religious faith in this fashion: "As to Jesus of Nazareth, . . . I have . . . some doubts as to his Divinity, tho' it is a question I do not dogmatize upon, having never studied it, and think it needless to busy myself with it now, when I expect soon an opportunity of knowing the truth with less trouble. I see no harm, however, in its being believed, if that belief has the good consequence . . . of making his doctrines more respected and better observed." We can understand Franklin's attitude and why he was willing to grant the widest latitude of belief to all men. The puzzling question is why many who were not religiously indifferent should have been equally ardent in the struggle for religious freedom. The answer is to be found in three fundamental theological convictions which were largely elaborated by the Independent party (Congregationalists and Baptists) during the English Civil War, 1642–48.

They were convinced, first of all, that *no mortal man and no human institution can be regarded as infallible*. As the Form of Government adopted by the Presbyterian Church in 1788 was to put it, even ecclesiastical assemblies are composed of "fallible men," and therefore it must be acknowledged that "all synods and councils may err through the frailty inseparable from humanity." Not even the self-disclosure of God in Scripture, John Calvin had insisted, could be regarded as self-explanatory. The understanding of divine truth is dependent upon the gift of the Holy Spirit, and no one can be absolutely certain of possessing the Spirit. Thus an element of humility and tentativeness must always be present. "We doubt not what we practice," said Thomas Hooker of Connecticut, "but it's beyond all doubt that all men are liars, and we are in the number of those poor feeble men; either we do or may err, though we do not know it; what we have learned we do profess, and profess still to live that we may learn."

From the 1640's on, there was an increasing insistence that the only way God's will could be disclosed and confirmed was through unfettered discussion. One Puritan leader asked "How can truth appear but by argumentation?" Another one wrote: "We have a proverb that they that will find must as well seek where a thing is not, as where it is. . . . And this liberty of free disquisition is as great a means to keep the truth as to find it. The running water keeps pure and clear, when the standing pool corrupts." God's will was made known through discussion because his Spirit was no respecter of persons. Light might break forth from "the meanest of the brethren." Truth might be perceived by any man. Every man, therefore, must be free to be convinced and in turn to convince.

Secondly, since they knew all men to be in bondage to sin and subject to the temptation to exalt themselves in rebellion against God, they insisted that *the church must be limited in power*. Human nature being what it is, all unchecked power could lead only to a defiance of God and a contemptuous indifference to the common good. Said John Cotton:

> Let all the world learn to give mortal man no greater power than they are content they shall use, for use it they will. . . . It is necessary . . . that all power that is on earth be limited, church power or other. . . . It is counted a matter of danger to the state to limit prerogatives, but it is a further danger not to have them limited.

As Cotton implied, the limitation of power is necessary in every area of life, and the experience of most early Americans had taught them that political and ecclesiastical absolutism were equally to be feared. Thus, while it was necessary to limit the power of the state, it was also necessary to limit the power of the church. Therefore, Cotton insisted that to give any power of coercion to the church would be to make "the church a monster." Governments, he continued, create a "monstrous deformity" when they surrender any of their authority to the church, so that if the church condemns anyone, they must do so too. It was for this reason that the Presbyterians were to state very explicitly that "ecclesiastical discipline" must not be "attended with any civil effects" and "can derive no force whatever but from its own justice, the approbation of an impartial public, and the countenance and blessing of the great Head of the Church Universal." The only power at the disposal of the church is the influence it may exert by persuasion.

Lastly, if the power of the church must be limited, *the church must also be free*—free to determine its own life, to define the basis of its membership, to speak God's word of judgment, to sound God's summons to repentance, to endeavor to shape the life of the total community according to its understanding of God's will. The church must be free to strive, however imperfectly, to be Christ's church. Christ is the head of the church, and Christ is the sole authority to which the church must yield obedience. To subject the church to the control and direction of the state, said Roger Williams in a tract which became a major manifesto of the Puritan Revolution, would be "to pull God and Christ and Spirit out of heaven, and subject them unto natural, sinful, inconstant men, and so consequently to Satan himself, by whom all peoples naturally are guided."

Even the best of men do not always see the full implications of their basic convictions, nor do they always live up to them. This was notably true of the New England Congregationalists, but even these New Englanders were never able to take active measures to suppress dissent without a lurking sense of guilt, as their involved casuistry makes clear. Freedom was not won without a struggle. But when freedom was denied, there were a host of men who responded as did Francis Makemie, when he declared: "To give bond not to preach . . . if invited by the people, we neither can nor dare do it." A right which is claimed for one's self, however, is not always extended to others. It was because men are fallible and inconstant, and because "God alone is Lord of the conscience," that the Presbyterians, for example, insisted that they did "not even wish to see any religious constitution aided by the civil power, further than may be necessary for protection and security." The sole responsibility of the state was to make sure that no one, "either upon pretense of religion or infidelity," be permitted "to offer any indignity, violence, abuse, or injury to any other person whatsoever," and to take proper precautions to insure that "all religious and ecclesiastical assemblies he held without molestation or disturbance." By the end of the colonial period, this was the common conviction of most American Protestants and it involved a forthright acceptance of the fact of Protestant diversity.

· 2 ·

THE COMMON HERITAGE

While American Protestantism was characterized from the very beginning by a multiplicity of independent groups, it was a multiplicity within an overarching unity. The Protestant churches of colonial America, of course, were first of all Christian churches, heirs of a tradition that ran back through the centuries to the earliest Christian communities. They were also Protestant churches, heirs of that decisive reordering or recovery of Christian tradition in the sixteenth-century Reformation. Furthermore, the overwhelming majority of these churches stood within a single Reformation tradition, and this predominant theological inheritance tended to set the tone and shape the views of all the churches. The common tradition was still further narrowed by the fact that the vast majority of the population of colonial America was British in background, with approximately 70 per cent at the time of the first census in 1790

being of English stock and an additional 15 per cent of Scottish
or Scotch-Irish descent. Finally, before the end of the colonial
period, all the churches to varying degrees had been further
molded to a common pattern by the pressures of the American
environment and by influences stemming from the Evangelical
Revival in eighteenth-century Britain and America.

The stamp of Geneva.—"The God most worshipped" in the
American colonies, Ralph Gabriel has reminded us, "was the
deity to whom John Calvin prayed with such intensity of devotion and singularity of purpose." It is important to remember
in this connection that the various Protestant groups did not
arrive at the same time, nor did they arrive in equal numbers.
Protestants who stood completely outside the Reformed or
Calvinist camp—Lutherans, Mennonites, Dunkers, and Moravians—made their appearance relatively late, and they were relatively few in numbers. With minor exceptions, the most significant being the Dutch Reformed, the non-British Protestant
groups did not arrive until the beginning of the eighteenth
century. By the end of the colonial period, Lutherans, Mennonites, Dunkers, and Moravians accounted for only 4.6 per cent
of the total number of Protestant congregations, while the Reformed groups from the Continent—the only other non-British
segment—constituted an additional 9 per cent. Both chrono-
logically and numerically, the predominant Old World religious
heritage in the American colonies was the Reformed or Calvinist
tradition as it found expression in English Puritanism and the
related Presbyterianism of Scotland and northern Ireland.

Anglicanism (the Church of England and the Protestant Episcopal Church in the United States) was the earliest form of
American Protestantism. Its beginnings date from the settlement at Jamestown in 1607. At the time of this initial settlement,

the Church of England was almost wholly Reformed in its theological orientation. The Calvinism of the *Institutes of the Christian Religion* was undoubtedly the predominant theological current, although the formulation of the Reformed faith by the Zurich reformer, Henry Bullinger, was widely influential and the impact of that variant form of Calvinism known as Arminianism was beginning to be felt. Furthermore, in Virginia as in England, there was strong Puritan or "low church" sentiment among the Anglicans. Prominent Puritans were directors of the Virginia Company, and Dale's Laws for regulating the religious and moral life of the colony have sometimes been described as having "out-Puritaned" Puritan New England. Alexander Whitaker was the best known of the early Anglican clergy, his zeal having won him the title "Apostle to Virginia." It was Whitaker, son of a noted Puritan professor at Cambridge University, who wrote the celebrated pamphlet *Good News from Virginia*. In a letter to a friend, he cited as a chief item of good news the fact that neither "subscription" nor "surplice"— points which were troubling Puritan consciences in England— were "spoken of" in Virginia. While this Puritan or "low church" trend was to be somewhat arrested in later years by the intervention of the bishop of London and by the activity of missionaries sent out by the Society for the Propagation of the Gospel, it was to receive new impetus toward the close of the colonial period by influences stemming from John Wesley.

Although Anglicanism was first in the field and although it was to have varying degrees of official support in all the colonies and was to be the established church in approximately half of them, it was never able fully to exploit its initial advantage. Too much has been made of the undoubted incompetence of some of the Anglican clergy. A more serious handicap was the lack of a bishop in America who could confirm and ordain, a handicap which made a fully developed church life impossible.

The three old denominations of English Dissent—Congregationalists, Presbyterians, and Baptists—were destined to play a much larger role than the Anglicans in the shaping of American Protestantism. By the end of the colonial period, the Congregationalists and the Presbyterians were the two largest religious groups, embracing about 40 per cent of all the churches. The Baptists ranked with the Anglicans in numerical importance, each representing about 15 per cent of the total number of congregations and presumably of adherents. These three groups —Congregationalists, Presbyterians, and Baptists—were linked by an essentially common confession of faith. The Congregationalists had accepted the Westminster Confession of Faith "for substance of doctrine" in 1648; the Presbyterians adopted it as their standard in 1729; and the major Baptist group adhered to it in a slightly altered form that included the substitution of the hyper-Calvinist triple covenant for the double covenant of the original confession.

The earliest Congregational churches date from the founding of Plymouth colony in 1620 and from the "great migration" to Massachusetts Bay which began in 1630. The intention of those engaged in the migration was to create "a city set on a hill" that would force, by the very power of its example, thoroughgoing religious reform at home. For a few brief years during the Puritan Revolution in England, it appeared that their expectation of producing sufficient ferment at home to effect the desired reform might be fulfilled, but the restoration of the Stuarts in 1660 demonstrated that this hope was illusory. New England rather than old England was to be the domain of Congregationalism; a land of small communities gathered about the village church.

Schools as well as churches were established, it being, as they put it, "one chief project of that old deluder Satan to keep men from the knowledge of the Scriptures." Their initial concern, however, had been to make immediate provision for the education of additional ministers, "dreading to leave an illiterate ministry to the churches when our present ministers shall lie in the dust." The founding of Harvard thus antedated the establishment in any systematic fashion, of primary and grammar schools, being accomplished within six years of the landing of the Winthrop fleet in 1630.

It was not the intent of the founders of New England to foster dissent, but it was here that Baptists and Presbyterians made their first appearance. Baptist beginnings date from the ejection of Roger Williams from Massachusetts Bay and his subsequent role in forming a Baptist church at Providence in 1639. While Rhode Island remained a center of Baptist activity, the major Baptist growth stemmed from the formation of the Philadelphia Baptist Association in 1707. This association, which was to embrace churches from Connecticut to Virginia and which founded Brown University as a training center for its ministers, carried on vigorous missionary activity from Nova Scotia to Georgia which was to result in a marked Baptist growth toward the close of the colonial period. Presbyterian beginnings closely paralleled those of the Baptists. Presbyterian sentiment was constantly cropping out in early New England and several Presbyterian churches were established by New Englanders, first on Long Island, and then in New Jersey, Pennsylvania, Maryland, and South Carolina. Several of these churches were brought together to form the Presbytery of Philadelphia in 1706. This early Presbyterianism was augmented numerically after 1710 by the great influx of Scotch-Irish population into the Middle colonies, the Piedmont region of the South, and the back country of New England.

The Quakers, who were widely dispersed throughout all the colonies, ranked fifth numerically among the colonial denominations, and their ethical and theological emphases betrayed many evidences of their origin within English Puritanism. They made their first appearance in the New World as itinerant "publishers of truth," and as early as 1656 two of these Quaker itinerants were imprisoned at Boston. West Jersey was the earliest Quaker colony, being under the control of Quaker proprietors from 1675 to 1692; and Quaker meetings had been formed in every colony from New Hampshire to South Carolina a full decade before Pennsylvania was founded in 1681.

Taken together, these five English-speaking denominations— Congregationalists, Presbyterians, Baptists, Anglicans, and Quakers—embraced 85 per cent of all the Protestant congregations at the time of the American Revolution. It was their predominance that accounts for many of the marked similarities of faith, practice, and outlook of the different Protestant churches in America. As the English language became the common language of all the colonists and as German and Dutch colonists joined with others in the American Revolution to defend their rights as Englishmen, so English patterns of church life tended to penetrate the churches of Continental origin. Gilbert Tennent, a Presbyterian, preached in Dutch Reformed pulpits. The early Swedish Lutherans along the Delaware and the French Reformed group in South Carolina both were absorbed into the Church of England, the German Lutherans—after an initial resistance led by Henry M. Muhlenberg—were to varying degrees Anglicized and Americanized.

From a theological point of view, however, it was the stamp

of Geneva which left the deepest mark upon American Protestantism during this early period, when it was being shaped to
a common pattern. This is not surprising in view of the fact that
the English-speaking churches were Calvinistic in background,
and were reinforced in this respect by the German, Dutch, and
French Reformed churches representing an additional 9 per
cent of the total number of congregations. It is even less surprising when one remembers that Calvinism was well adapted to
the needs of men struggling to tame a wilderness. Sturdy virtues
were demanded by the hard conditions of life in the New
World, and these virtues were supplied by a religious faith
[whic]h spoke to men in terms of stern imperatives and high des-
[ti]nd expressed itself most characteristically in terms of rest-
[less e]nergy, unfaltering confidence, and unblinking acceptance
[of th]e harsh facts of life. The end result of this process of pene-
[trat]ion was noted by a British visitor who commented that
[A]merica is not a melting-pot at all, she is merely a varnishing
[po]t, from which a thin veneer of seventeenth century English
[P]uritanism has been laid over the most diverse religious tradi-
[ti]ons."

It was no thin veneer, however, which bound the major colonial denominations together. John Witherspoon, the most famous colonial Presbyterian leader, in commenting upon the religious situation in New Jersey at the close of the American
Revolution, remarked that "Baptists are Presbyterians in all
other respects, differing only in the point of infant baptism;
their political weight goes the same way as the Presbyterians."
By this observation, Witherspoon was simply pointing up the
evident fact that the larger religious bodies were cut to a common pattern. In this particular instance, the respective doctrinal
standards—the Westminster Confession of Faith and the Phila-

delphia Confession of Faith—were almost identical, forms of worship were the same, moral attitudes and political convictions were similar, and differences of church government apparently were not regarded by him to be sufficiently significant to be worth noting. Baptists, of course, had been moving in the direction of a stronger and more centralized denominational life, whereas some of the more rigid features of Presbyterian polity had been softened by Scottish and American experience. As for Presbyterians and Congregationalists, their community of interest and identity was even more striking. The election of Jonathan Edwards, a Congregationalist, to the presidency of Presbyterian Princeton was a conspicuous illustration of the ease with which ministers moved back and forth between the two groups. In many ways, during the later colonial period, the two denominations were almost indistinguishable, and the intimate and cordial relationship which existed between them was to culminate in the adoption of a Plan of Union in 1801.

The influence of the environment.—While colonial Protestantism was partly the product of influences stemming from Geneva, it was also shaped to a common pattern by circumstances of life in a new land. Crèvecœur, in commenting upon the American scene, noted that the American had become a new creature in the process of being transplanted from the Old World to the New. This subtle transformation occasioned by a change of environment was no less true of the churches. They found themselves in a situation in which many of their inherited practices and procedures were not readily applicable and offered them no clear guidance. A long sea journey had left them largely on their own amid the vast spaces and primitive setting of an empty continent. Thus, confronted by immediate and urgent needs, they were forced to improvise and adapt and adjust as best they could. Captain John Smith described how, in Virginia, they had had to "make do" in providing a place of worship.

When I first went to Virginia, I well remember we did hang an awning (which is an old sail) to three or four trees to shadow us from the sun, our walls were rails of wood, our seats unhewed trees till we cut planks, our pulpit a bar of wood nailed to two neighboring trees. In foul weather, we shifted into an old rotten tent, for we had few better. . . . This was our church, till we built a homely thing like a barn.

It was also frequently necessary to "make do" in terms of organizational procedure. The Reverend Jonas Michaelius of New Amsterdam noted this fact in 1628 when he explained to his brethren back home the reason for the irregularities which attended the formation of his church. "One cannot," he informed them, "observe strictly all the usual formalities in making a beginning under such circumstances." In New England, one such forced departure from traditional practice was defended by John Allin as being not necessarily irregular, since "it is the way of Christ in the Gospel to set up the practice of his institutions as the necessities of the people call for them." Whether it was the way of Christ or not, the "necessities" of life in the colonies did remold and reshape the churches.

One of the consequences of the shift to the new environment was the decisive voice which the laity began to exercise in the determination of church affairs. This movement toward lay control can scarcely be regarded as a surprising development, for the early ministers were far removed from the status-giving context of an ordered church life and were largely dependent upon the support they could marshal among the laity both for the formation and maintenance of a particular church. Under these conditions, the ministerial office conferred little authority beyond that personal authority which a minister might be able to command by virtue of his own character, wisdom, ability, and example. Henry M. Muhlenberg made this discovery when he arrived from Germany in 1742 with the intention of reducing the newly formed Lutheran churches to some degree of ecclesiastical order. "A preacher," he confessed, "must fight his way through with the Sword of the Spirit alone and depend upon faith in the living God and his promises, if he wants to be a preacher [in America]." Even in New England, where the early Congregational churches had been properly constituted with due recognition being given to ministerial authority, this state of affairs did not long endure. The Congregational conception of the ministry as "a speaking aristocracy," having powers independent of the laity, suffered rapid erosion—presumably as a result of the tough-grained individualism fostered by the hard conditions of life in a frontier society—so that the ministers, as Perry Miller has observed, were soon "shorn of every weapon except moral persuasion." Among the Anglican churches of Virginia, the same process was at work, with actual control falling into the hands of lay vestries which had the power to hire the minister and to determine his salary, this control being justified by noting that "the parishioners were the founders of the churches, having built and endowed them."

A second circumstance which tended to shape all the churches to a common pattern was the simple fact that in the New World a new beginning had to be made. This new beginning at the outset involved the formation of local congregations which only later could be drawn into traditional synodical, diocesan, or associational relationships. Thus the transplanted churches, whatever their traditional polity, tended to become independent self-governing units which resisted subsequent attempts to regularize their status by subordinating them to a wider ecclesiastical jurisdiction. The Anglicans, for example, were never able to establish an episcopate in America throughout the whole colonial period, and much of the opposition to the completion of the church by the creation of American bishops came from within their own ranks. William White, who was himself destined to become a bishop after the close of the American Revolution, declared in 1782 that "there cannot be produced an instance of laymen in America, unless in the very infancy of the settlements, soliciting the introduction of a bishop." The "great majority" of the laity, he continued, were convinced that it would be "an hazardous experiment" which would jeopardize their prerogatives. A similar spirit manifested itself among the Congregationalists of Massachusetts Bay, where the proposal to complete the Congregational structure with a yearly consultative synod was rejected out of hand by the deputies of the General Court. The Presbyterians, to be sure, were able to establish presbyteries and synods. But it also should be remembered that, as a result of "the struggle for dominance between synod and presbytery," the presbytery won the crucial right of control over examination for ordination. This represented a victory for a kind of localism, for one presbytery in an ordination examination could emphasize Christian experience as the important qualification and another could stress correctness of doctrine. Furthermore, the controversies of the eighteenth century demonstrated that even a local Presbyterian congregation could successfully defy control from above if it was determined to have its own way.

The breakdown of the parish system, by which a whole community was embraced within the church and subjected to its discipline, was another casualty of the shift from the Old World to the New. In Virginia it was the pattern of settlement that constituted the major difficulty. How could the parish system be adapted to a population thinly distributed on large plantations along the whole length of navigable rivers? How could a clergyman expect to conduct even the routine affairs of the church in a parish that might be a hundred miles in length? How could he even hope to keep in touch with his parishioners, to say nothing of maintaining the discipline of the church among them? In 1661 the author of *Virginia's Cure* acknowledged that the great problem was the "scattered planting" of the population and argued that the only remedy was to reduce the "planters into towns." He proposed that money should be raised in England for the purpose of building towns in every county of Virginia. The planters could then be made to bring their families and servants to those centers on weekends so that they could be subjected to regular catechetical instruction and church attendance. This proposal, as Sidney E. Mead has suggested, was the counsel of an ardent but obviously despairing churchman.

Elsewhere in the colonies the abandonment of the effort to impose and maintain religious uniformity sounded the death knell to the parish system, which presupposed that the whole community would belong to a single church. In most of the colonies the churches were "gathered" churches from the start. Only in New England did the religious homogeneity of the population and the pattern of settlement on small landholdings gathered together into closely knit towns permit anything that even resembled the parish system to be established. Even so, the successful operation of the parish system in New England involved a modification of the Congregationalist insistence that only those who could give some evident proofs of grace should belong to the church. In the very earliest years, when the total population was largely a "sifted" people, the traditional Congregationalist conception of the church posed no great problem, but a problem did arise when the children of believers were unable to report having experienced the miracle of grace and thus were not able to qualify for church membership. This posed a very real threat to the parish system which was dependent upon the church embracing at least the larger portion of the population, and this threat to the parish system was the "necessity" which led John Allin to justify the adoption of a "half-way" covenant by which the children of unregenerate children of believers might be baptized and brought within the scope of the church's discipline. It was by this expedient that the collapse of the parish system in New England was deferred until the inroads of dissent dashed all hopes of maintaining it unimpaired. When Jonathan Edwards in the 1730's abandoned the effort to preserve the parish structure and insisted that Congregationalists must return to their initial emphasis upon the church as a covenanted community of convinced believers, he was only recognizing what had become a new "necessity" in terms of the actualities of the changed situation.

Thus, long before the end of the colonial period, all the churches—whatever their traditional polity may have been—had become in effect "gathered" churches with a strong emphasis upon local autonomy and lay control.

The impact of Evangelicalism.—A further influence shaping the life of the American churches during the colonial period was the appearance in both Britain and America of that type of religious vitality and fervor which is most closely associated in the popular mind with the rise of Methodism. In the colonies it produced the sweeping tide of revivals during the eighteenth century which became known as the Great Awakening. Evangelicalism, to use the term by which this new surge of spiritual life is more properly designated, has often been pictured as a revolt against Calvinism, but it was scarcely that in the beginning. The ordered theological system of Calvinism was largely taken for granted, and most of the leaders regarded themselves as good Calvinists. John Wesley, to be sure, entered a vigorous dissent at the point of predestination, but in most respects he stood fully within the theological tradition that stemmed from Geneva. Evangelicalism, however, was much more a mood and an emphasis than a theological system. Its stress was upon the importance of a personal religious or conversion experience. If it was a revolt against anything, it was a revolt against the notion that the Christian life involved little more than observing the outward formalities of religion.

The fact that most of the colonial population stood outside the churches altogether and could only be brought into the "gathered" churches by whatever powers of persuasion they were able to exert made it almost inevitable that something analogous to the emphasis of Evangelicalism should make its appearance among them. There was scant prospect that even the formalities of religion would continue to be observed in the American colonies because of the absence of the social control exerted by custom and tradition in older communities. Thus the churches were confronted by a clear-cut summons to missionary endeavor. The great need was to reach the unchurched, and—given the circumstances of colonial society—this called for a type of preaching that would prick the conscience, convict men of sin, and lead them through a crisis of individual decision into a personal experience of God's redeeming love.

The Great Awakening began in 1726 with the revivalistic preaching of Theodore J. Frelinghuysen, the pastor of four Dutch Reformed churches in New Jersey, and it soon made its appearance among the Presbyterians through the instrumentality of Frelinghuysen's neighbor, Gilbert Tennent, the young Presbyterian pastor in New Brunswick. The earliest manifestation of the revival among New England Congregationalists occurred at Northampton in 1734 under the preaching of Jonathan Edwards, whose *Faithful Narrative of the Surprising Work of God* (1737) was to have a profound influence upon the Wesleys and was to do much to stylize the pattern of future revivals. In the South, the Awakening went through three phases. The initial phase was a Presbyterian revival initiated by men from the New Brunswick Presbytery in New Jersey. The second phase was a back-country revival under the leadership of Shubal Stearns, a "separate" Baptist from New England. The final phase, on the eve of the American Revolution, was a typically Methodist development among the Anglicans, stemming largely from the influence of Devereux Jarratt, an evangelical-minded rector in Dinwiddie County, Virginia. While many of the leaders of the Awakening moved from colony to colony, the great figure that linked the local revivals into a single movement was George Whitefield, who made repeated preaching expeditions up and down the coast from Georgia to New Hampshire.

The Awakening was not greeted with equal enthusiasm by everyone. There were many who were disturbed by the irregularities and excesses of the revivalists. The initial consequence, therefore, was to divide the churches into revivalist and antirevivalist parties—into "New Sides" and "Old Sides" among the Presbyterians, and into "New Lights" and "Old Lights" among the Congregationalists. A sermon by Gilbert Tennent on the "Danger of an Unconverted Ministry" in 1740 led to a formal division among the Presbyterians the following year. But, when the two groups reunited in 1758 to form the Synod of New York and Philadelphia, the New Side had increased fourfold while the Old Side had not even held its own. The revivalists were equally victorious among the Dutch Reformed, but in New England their opponents were able to command a majority to condemn their "errors in doctrine and disorders in practice." There was a tendency in many of the New England Congregational churches for the revivalist minority to withdraw and form "separate" churches of their own. The major effect of the withdrawal was to contribute greatly to Baptist growth, since many of these "separate" Congregational churches tended to become Baptist. Yet, even among the New England Congregationalists, the revivalists ultimately won the day, persuading even the Old Lights to adopt the techniques developed in the Awakening.

The revival, of course, was not restricted to the colonies. There were many scattered "awakenings" of new religious life in the eighteenth century—in England, Scotland, and Wales, as well as in America. Whether they are to be regarded as a renewal of Puritan "experimental" religion or traced to Pietistic influences from the Continent is not of great moment. It can be argued, with good reason, that the revivals began in the American colonies with the preaching of Frelinghuysen, then spread to England through the activity and influence of George Whitefield, and returned once again through Wesleyan converts to strengthen the new life that had come out of the Great Awakening in America. But whatever direction the reciprocal influences took, it is clear that men of all denominations were caught up in the movement. And the churches of all denominations were profoundly affected by its impact. The structure of public worship was modified, a more popular type of preaching dominated the pulpit, new forms of architecture were introduced, and even the churches' understanding of their mission was altered. So pervasive was to be its influence that William Warren Sweet asserted that these revivals "marked the beginning of what might be termed the peculiar American emphasis in Christianity," while a Presbyterian historian, noting their continuing impact upon the life of the churches of all denominations, called the nineteenth century "the Methodist age" of American church history.

· 3 ·

THE CONCEPT OF DENOMINATIONALISM

The whole structure of American Protestantism rests upon a particular understanding of the nature of the Church—the denominational theory of the Church. The use of the word "denomination" to describe a religious group came into vogue during the early years of the Evangelical Revival. Typical of the mood which gave currency to the new term were John Wesley's oft-quoted words: "I . . . refuse to be distinguished from other men by any but the common principles of Christianity. . . . I renounce and detest all other marks of distinction. But from real Christians, of whatever *denomination*, I earnestly desire not to be distinguished at all. . . . Dost thou love and fear God? It is enough! I give thee the right hand of fellowship." The word denomination was adopted by the leaders of the Evangelical Revival, both in England and America, because it carried with it no implication of a negative value judgment.

Denominationalism is the opposite of sectarianism. A "sect" claims the authority of Christ for itself alone. By definition a sect is exclusive—separate. The word "denomination," on the other hand, is an inclusive term—an ecumenical term. It implies that the group referred to is but one member, called or *denominated* by a particular name, of a larger group—the Church—to which all denominations belong. The basic contention of the denominational theory of the Church is that the true Church is not to be identified exclusively with any single ecclesiastical structure. No denomination claims to represent the whole Church of Christ. No denomination claims that all other churches are false churches. Each denomination is regarded as constituting a different "mode" of expressing in the outward forms of worship and organization that larger life of the Church in which they all share.

The denominational theory of the Church was well adapted to the situation in which the Protestants of colonial America found themselves as they moved into the eighteenth century. They were confronted by a situation in which the vast majority of the population stood outside the churches altogether. The great need was for the various churches to co-operate with one another, in freedom and mutual respect, in the great task of reducing the rest of society to Christian obedience. It was this that the denominational theory of the Church, by emphasizing their essential unity while giving due recognition to their diversity, permitted them to do in good conscience. The phrase "in good conscience" is important, for this understanding of the nature of the Church was not a mere pragmatic adjustment to the necessities of a practical situation. It was a conception which had deep roots in the Protestant tradition.

The teaching of the Reformers.—While the term "denomination" was popularized by the leaders of the eighteenth-century Awakening, the theory it represented had been hammered out by a group of Puritan divines in the preceding century who in turn, were largely indebted to the Protestant Reformers of the sixteenth century for their fundamental insights.

The insistence that the true Church can never be identified in any exclusive sense with a particular ecclesiastical institution was one of the basic affirmations of the Reformers. Neither the continuity nor the unity of the Church, they asserted, depends ultimately upon outward ecclesiastical forms. The true succession is a succession of believers, and the real unity is the unity to be found wherever faith has been awakened. Luther's fundamental criticism of his opponents was his contention that they sought to imprison Christ within man-made historical forms. Although it is inevitable and necessary that the Church find institutional expression "in a place and in the things and activities of the world," said Luther, "yet in this life the Church is not properly understood in terms of all this." It should be remembered that "as in this life the Church is not without eating and drinking and yet the Kingdom of God, according to Paul, does not consist of eating and drinking, so the Church is not without place and body and yet the place and body do not make the Church and do not constitute it." The external ecclesiastical arrangements ought to be of such an order that they do not block the free course of the Word of God in the world, but Luther never doubted that men could be found by Christ even under conditions in which he was misinterpreted and the gospel

35

perverted and defiled. Calvin was more convinced than Luther that external ecclesiastical arrangements were prescribed in Scripture, but he had a word of caution for those who "are not satisfied unless the Church can always be pointed out with the finger." This, he insisted in the preface to the *Institutes*, is something which cannot be done in any final sense. The whole question of the dimensions, the boundaries, the limits of the Church of Christ must be left to God, "since he alone 'knoweth them that are his.'"

Luther and Calvin made use of this insight only to a limited degree. It was a useful instrument for the criticism of others, but the broad-minded spirit it implied found only partial positive expression. The Reformers, as a whole, were willing to recognize as true churches all churches that possessed an essentially evangelical faith whether they were Lutheran churches in Germany and Scandinavia; Reformed churches in Switzerland, Holland, and Scotland; or an Anglican church in England. All these churches in their various geographical areas were seen as differing manifestations of the one holy catholic Church which embraced them all. But the Reformers hesitated when there was religious diversity within a particular geographical area rather than between different geographical areas. They were firmly convinced that there must be religious uniformity within a particular political jurisdiction. For this reason, they found it difficult to accept the notion that churches of differing church order located on opposite corners in the same city could be regarded as sharing in the life of the whole Church. Yet this latter view was implicit in the whole structure of Reformation thinking concerning the nature of the Church. It was left for a later generation to point out that so long as men live "in this muddy world" and so long as "deceitfulness" lurks within the human heart, it will be impossible for men to dogmatize concerning their apprehensions of the way in which Christ would have them walk, and that it is therefore necessary to recognize that even those who feel compelled to walk separately in obedience to Christ are united by a bond which transcends their divisions.

The architects of the denominational theory.—The real architects of the denominational theory of the Church were the seventeenth-century Independent divines within the Church of England, whose most prominent representatives were the Dissenting Brethren in the Westminster Assembly. These men had been in exile on the Continent during the years preceding the Puritan Revolution, but when the issue between king and parliament was joined, they returned to participate in the struggle and to help remodel the English church. While in exile abroad, they had been forced to inquire, as they put it, into the positive part of church government. They believed that being completely on their own had freed them from bias and thus had allowed them to search out the proper pattern of church government with impartiality, being guided only by the "light and touch" of God's Spirit.

> We had, of all men, the greatest reason to be true to our own consciences . . . , seeing that it was for our conscience that we were deprived at once of whatever was dear to us. We had no new commonwealths to rear to frame the church unto. . . . We had no state-ends or political interests to comply with; no kingdoms in our eye to subdue to our mold . . . ; no preferments or worldly respects to shape our opinion for. We had nothing else to do but simply and singly to consider how to worship God acceptably and so most according to his Word.

They freely acknowledged that they could not profess such "sufficiency of knowledge" as to be able to "lay forth all those

37

rules" contained in Scripture, but they were confident that they had found "principles enough, . . . to us clear and certain, and such as might well serve to preserve our churches in peace and from offense and would comfortably guide us to heaven in a safe way."

When the Westminster Assembly was summoned by Parliament in 1643 to propose a new form of government for the English church, these former exiles were sufficiently confident of the correctness of their views to be eager to persuade the Assembly to adopt them as the basis for remodeling the established church. They professed their willingness, however, to listen with open minds to the other members of the Assembly. In spite of the favorable situation for impartial inquiry in which they had found themselves as a result of exile, they remembered, they said, "our own frailty in the former way of our conformity" and therefore they were ready to "alter or retract" whatever was shown to be derived from a misunderstanding of Scripture.

Thus far the Dissenting Brethren were simply echoing the point of view which had been expressed in 1639 by their fellow Congregationalists in Massachusetts Bay when responding to an inquiry concerning their ecclesiastical practice.

We see as much cause to suspect the integrity of our own hearts as yours; and so much the more, as being more privy to the deceitfulness of our own hearts than to yours . . . , which causeth us with great reverence to accept and receive what further light God may be pleased to impart unto us by you. But as we have believed, so have we hitherto practiced. . . . If anything appear to be unsound and dissonant from the Word, which we for our parts cannot discern, we shall willingly attend to what further light God may send unto us by you.

Thomas Hooker in Connecticut prefaced his description of the Congregational "way," in *A Survey of the Sum of Church Discipline*, with the acknowledgment that his "only aim" was to lay down "the grounds of our practice according to that measure of light I have received" in the hope that this "might occasion men eminently gifted to make further search and to dig deeper that, if there be any vein of reason which lies yet lower, it might be brought to light." "We profess and promise," he continued, "not only a ready ear to hear it, but a heart willing to welcome it."

Unfortunately the "further search" in which these men professed themselves ready to engage did not result in the achievement of a common mind with regard to the form of church government that should replace the uprooted prelacy. Differences of opinion proved to be less easily resolved than either the Congregationalists in New England or the Dissenting Brethren in the Westminster Assembly had so confidently assumed. The Puritan party in England, which had been so firmly united in its opposition to the conformity imposed by "lordly bishops," turned out to be badly fragmented when agreement was sought on specific proposals for the reform of the established church. Some of the Puritans were for a moderate episcopacy; some were for a presbyterian establishment; some, like the Dissenting Brethren, were for a congregational form of church government; and some were beginning to advocate the restriction of church membership to those who had been baptized as believers. The Dissenting Brethren could neither persuade the others that they were mistaken, nor could they themselves be persuaded that they were wrong. It was at this juncture that the Dissenting Brethren formulated the denominational theory of the church as a way out of the impasse in which the Puritan party found itself.

The Westminster Assembly met in the midst of a civil war (1642–49), and the Dissenting Brethren were keenly aware of "the danger of rending and dividing the godly Protestant party" at a time when there was "an absolute necessity of their nearest union and conjunction." But it was not simply that division threatened the cause of those who were desirous of a godly reformation, it represented a denial of the whole spirit of Christianity. "We are wrangling, devising, plotting, working against one another, minding nothing but to get the day of one another," said Jeremiah Burroughes, whereas "love and unity are Christ's badge, the arms of a Christian, whereby he shows of what house he is." It is an unhappy fact, he continued, that "we are divided notwithstanding we are all convinced of the evil of our divisions. We cry out exceedingly against them . . . , yet scarce a man does anything . . . towards any help against divisions or furtherance of our union." It would be easy enough, of course, to secure unity "if those who differ from others would give up their judgments and practices to them, to believe what they believe, and to do what they do." But, said Burroughes, this they cannot do, for "Christ hath laid this charge upon [his followers] . . . that they must not believe anything in matters of religion but what they shall first see ground for out of his Word." The problem, he asserted, was to find a way to unity when Christians do not all agree. "If we stay for peace and love till we come to the unity of the faith in all things, we must stay, for ought I know, till we come to another world. . . . The unity of the faith and the perfect man will both be together."

The case for denominationalism.—If Christians are to be

united, "notwithstanding their differences," there are several fundamental truths which these seventeenth-century divines insisted they must accept.

First of all, "considering the wants and weaknesses that do ordinarily attend men's apprehensions," it is inevitable that there should be differences of opinion about the implications of the Christian faith for the outward life of the church. Christians in all ages have differed in judgment about the patterns of organization and worship that best serve to express and safeguard the Christian faith. Even the Apostles could not in their time wholly prevent such differences from arising.

In the second place, even though these differences of opinion do not involve the fundamentals of the faith, they are not matters of mere indifference. Every Christian is under obligation to practice as he believes and to pursue to the end the implications of the convictions he honestly holds. To insist that he submit to the judgment of other men is to allow other men to become lords of his conscience, but those who fear God must first be persuaded themselves before they can accept another man's judgment.

It should be further recognized that differences of opinion, honestly held, can lead to profitable and fruitful discussion out of which a fuller apprehension of truth may emerge. We must not forget, said Burroughes, that God may have a hand in our divisions to bring forth further light, for "sparks are beaten out by the flints striking together." How can men "know they are right . . . , till they—by discussing, praying, reading, meditating—find that out"?

Moreover, since no church has a final and unambiguous grasp of divine truth, the true Church of Christ can never be fully represented by any single ecclesiastical structure. God is not the exclusive possession of any church, and the existence of different churches—each striving to the best of its understanding to be a faithful and worthy representation of Christ's Church in the life of the world—serves as a constant corrective to the pretensions of all churches. By this means and by their mutual criticism, the tendency of all religious institutions to absolutize themselves is checked.

Furthermore, the unity that does exist among the godly, in spite of their differences, must not be forgotten.

> Though our differences are sad enough, yet they come not up to this to make us men of different religions. We agree in the same end, though not in the same means. They are but different ways of opposing the common enemy. The agreeing in the same means, in the same way of opposing the common enemy, would be very comfortable. It would be our strength. But that cannot be expected in this world.

The actual fact is that "our divisions have been and still are between good men," and it is equally true that "there are as many godly Presbyterians as Independents." This means that, "though we are fully persuaded by God's Word and Spirit that this our Way is Christ's Way, yet we neither do nor dare judge others to be reprobates that walk not with us in it, but leave all judgment to God, and heartily pray for them."

Finally, it is necessary to remember that the mere fact of separation does not of itself constitute schism. "Though they may be divided from such a particular society, yet they are not divided from the Church," for "the true nature of schism is . . . an uncharitable, unjust, rash, violent breaking from union with the church or members of it." To those who cry out against every separation, even when "loving and peaceable," as constituting schism, Burroughes made a detailed reply. He pointed out that refugee groups from abroad and Scots from north of the Tweed had been permitted to have their own churches in England because they "could not acknowledge the bishops' authority nor communicate in the sacraments in the parishes where they lived without sin to them," yet they were not charged with being schismatics. Furthermore, it was perfectly lawful for a man to have the liberty of "choosing pastors" by "choosing houses," moving from one parish where in good conscience he could not enjoy the means of grace to another parish where he could; and when he does so, no cry of schism is raised against him. It is not "the allowance of the state" that makes these instances no schism, said Burroughes, for "if it be schism . . . without the allowance of the state . . . , it is schism when the state does allow it."

> When men, who give good testimony of their godliness and peaceableness, . . . cannot without sin to them (though it be through weakness) enjoy all the ordinances of Christ and partake in all the duties of worship as members of that congregation where there dwelling is, they therefore in all humility and meekness . . . join in another congregation, yet . . . not condemning those churches they join not with as false but still preserve all Christian communion with the saints as members of the same body of Christ, of the Church Catholic, and join also with them in all duties . . . so far as they are able—if this be called schism, it is more than yet I have learned.

What the Dissenting Brethren wanted was "the peaceable practices of our consciences" which the Reformed churches abroad had allowed them as exiles. But they wanted more than that. They were pleading for that which to them was much more important—the establishment of the type of relationship among the differing Puritan groups in England which had existed between the Dissenting Brethren and the Reformed churches abroad, where "we both mutually gave and received the right hand of fellowship," recognizing, as Henry Burton was to put it, that "the Catholic Church . . . includes all true churches throughout the world."

When it is remembered that, although Christians may be divided at many points, they are nonetheless united in Christ, it then becomes possible, Burroughes insisted, for them to work together for the common ends of "godliness." After all, is it not true that "soldiers who march against a common enemy all under the same captain, who follow the same colors in their ensign and wear them upon their hats or arms, may get the day though they be not all clothed alike, though they differ in things of less concernment"? What is required of the Christian is to "join with all our might in all we know, and with peaceable, quiet, humble spirits seek to know more, and in the meantime carry ourselves humbly and peaceably toward those we differ from, and Christ will not charge us at the Great Day for retarding his cause."

The denominational theory in colonial America.—The restoration of the Stuarts in 1660 marked the collapse of Oliver Cromwell's attempt to give concrete expression to the denominational theory in his "voluntary national establishment," but the defeat was only temporary. Not only did the repressive legislation of the Clarendon code keep alive the sense of a common cause among the Nonconformist groups; the fundamental convictions of the Dissenting Brethren concerning the nature of the Church penetrated the thinking even of members of the episcopate, and thus smoothed the way for the adoption of the Act of Toleration in 1689. So thoroughly was the victory won that the leaders of the Evangelical Revival in England and

America could take the denominational conception of the Church largely for granted. Stiff-necked sectarians, to be sure, were to be found among all the Protestant bodies, but as the colonial period moved toward its close their point of view had become increasingly anachronistic. The future belonged to the colonial revivalists who had been nurtured by such writings as Henry Scougal's *The Life of God in the Soul of Man,* which reminded them that they must not mistake the trappings of religion for religion itself. The stress was upon inward religious experience as fundamental to the Christian life, and that which was of central importance, therefore, was the work of grace in the individual believer.

The denominational theory of the Church, by acknowledging the unity which existed within the diversity of outward ecclesiastical forms, made it possible for the colonial revivalists to make a concerted response to the missionary summons implicit in a situation in which the vast majority of the population stood outside the churches altogether. These revivalists were ready to preach in meetinghouses of various denominations, and they were not unduly disturbed when their converts chose to relate themselves to a denomination other than their own. George Whitefield was perhaps the greatest of the colonial revivalists, and his spirit was typical of them all. Preaching from a balcony in Philadelphia, he raised his eyes to the heavens and cried out:

Father Abraham, whom have you in heaven? Any Episcopalians? No! Any Presbyterians? No! Any Independents or Methodists? No, no, no! Whom have you there? We don't know those names here. All who are here are Christians. . . . Oh, is this the case? Then God help us to forget party names and to become Christians in deed and truth.

Samuel Davies, leader of the Presbyterian revival in the South and later president of Princeton, expressed a similar sentiment when he said:

My brethren, I would now warn you against this wretched, mischievous spirit of party. . . . A Christian! a christian! let that be your highest distinction; let that be the name which you labor to deserve. God forbid that my ministry should be the occasion of diverting your attention to anything else. . . . It has . . . been the great object of my zeal to inculcate upon you the grand essentials of our holy religion, and make you sincere, practical Christians. Alas! . . . unless I succeed in this, I labor to very little purpose, though I should presbyterianize the whole colony.

The concept of the Church which underlay this broad-minded spirit had been given explicit statement somewhat earlier by Gilbert Tennent. "All societies," he declared, "who profess Christianity and retain the foundational principles thereof, notwithstanding their different denominations and diversity of sentiments in smaller things, are in reality but one Church of Christ, but several branches (more or less pure in minuter points) of one visible kingdom of the Messiah." This was to be the characteristic emphasis throughout the nineteenth century. In spite of rivalries between denominations and occasional excesses of party zeal, the major Protestant bodies were to be firmly wedded to the denominational principle.

This lenient attitude was not born of doctrinal laxity and indifference, nor was it extended to all religious professions. While the major Protestant bodies were ready—for good theological reasons—to grant to others the liberty they claimed for themselves, the sense of being one Church in differing manifestations was restricted to those who shared a common understanding of the core of the Christian faith. These were the "evangelical" Christians, and those who did not share their basic convictions—the Unitarians and Universalists at a later date, for example—stood outside the camp. But, since a firm belief in the natural depravity of man was part of that necessary core of doctrine, they regarded it as hopeless to expect even the godly to agree in all things. Where they differed on the implications of the Christian faith for the outward form of the Church, they must in obedience to Christ go their separate ways. On the other hand, excessive scrupulosity and sectarian bickering, which elevated subordinate convictions to the level of the "grand essentials" of the Christian faith, was only evidence of an unregenerate heart.

The denominational theory which permitted the colonial Protestants to express their basic unity in the midst of their obvious diversity was not without its dangers. As the principle of religious liberty is misapplied when it is transferred from the civil to the ecclesiastical realm, thus making ecclesiastical discipline impossible and leaving a church with no confession to make to the world, so also the denominational theory contains within it the same reductionist potential. As a means of expressing theologically the unity that existed among the major Protestant bodies, the denominational theory enabled them to co-operate in good conscience for the achievement of those great ends which they had in common. The great temptation, however, was to transform the denominational theory from a means of expressing unity into a means of securing unity—to seek to enlist all men of good will under the banner of righteousness by a progressive narrowing of the central core of the Christian faith until little remained that was theologically incisive or distinctively Christian. Thus it was a precarious balance that American Protestants were called upon to maintain with their concept of denominationalism. The concept was designed to serve them as a counter to sectarian dogmatism and exclusiveness while, at the same time, avoiding the evil of indifference. By its very nature, this was a posture which required a considerable measure of theological sophistication to maintain without slipping into the perils on either side. Since such sophistication was not always present, the successes and failures in maintaining the precarious balance between dogmatism and indifference were destined to become one of the major themes in the story of American Protestantism.

Shaping a Protestant America

1787-1914

The winning of independence severed the ties which bound the colonies to the British crown, but seven years of war left the former colonists exhausted, impoverished, and disorganized. They were conscious of having brought a new nation into existence, but competing loyalties to local interests still persisted. As a consequence, they were fearful lest they find themselves unable to marshal the political wisdom and the popular support necessary to effect an enduring union.

Protestant churchmen were not less anxious than the rest of the population. They had the additional concern that the new nation should become a godly society. Moreover, they were conscious of a new and broader responsibility devolving upon the churches of a self-governing nation. Previously many aspects of the life of the individual colonies had been perforce determined by the authorities at home. Now the destiny of a whole nation was in American hands to the extent that God, by his favor or displeasure, permitted them to determine it; and the leaders of the churches were haunted by the prospect that both people and churches might fail to measure up to the responsibility that had been imposed upon them.

The anxiety of the churchmen was heightened by the low ebb of religious life. The great revivals which had served to strengthen all the churches had come to an end, and it was the war rather than religion which had elicited fervor and excitement. "A state of war," Benjamin Trumbull—looking back in 1818 to the post-Revolutionary years—noted in his *History of Connecticut,*

is peculiarly unfriendly to religion. It dissipates the mind, diminishes the degree of instruction, removes great numbers almost wholly from it, connects them with the most dangerous company, and presents them with the worst examples. It hardens and emboldens men in sin; is productive of profaneness, intemperance, disregard to propriety, violence, and licentious living.

In similar vein, Timothy Dwight commented in a letter to a contemporary that the Revolutionary War "unhinged the principles, the morality, and the religion of this country more than could have been done by a peace of forty years." Furthermore, in addition to conventional irreligion, there was a new "free-thinking" spirit—French "infidelity," they were later to call it—abroad in the land. This spirit, with its rejection of revealed religion, intensified the sense of foreboding among churchmen about the future of the nation.

But before the Protestant churches could launch the powerful counteroffensive to win the new nation to Christian obedience, they had to resolve institutional problems of their own. Church life had been disrupted by the war, and in the religious ebb tide of the immediate postwar years it was by no means obvious that the churches would be able to survive.

· 4 ·

THE CHURCHES IN THE POST-REVOLUTIONARY ERA

All the churches had been affected by the general impoverishment and disorganization of the war years, and the winning of independence created new problems for them. Ministers had marched off to become chaplains or "fighting parsons." Synods and associations frequently had been unable to meet. The different denominational groups, to be sure, had survived the Revolution with varying fortunes—Anglicans, Quakers, Mennonites, and Moravians having suffered most; and Congregationalists, Presbyterians, and Baptists least. After the war, those churches which had been linked to ecclesiastical bodies abroad had to fashion ecclesiastical structures of their own, while those which had been organized on a colonial basis were confronted with the need for a national organization.

Congregationalists, Presbyterians, and Baptists.—The Congregationalists and Presbyterians were the two largest colonial denominations, and they emerged from the war with the prestige which came from having given solid support to the Revolutionary cause. These two groups, for the most part, had come to regard themselves as a single phalanx, with a regional allocation of territory. The Scotch-Irish Presbyterians who settled in the back country of New England were largely absorbed into the Congregational churches, while the Congregationalists who moved southward tended, almost without exception, to

51

become Presbyterians; and this relationship had been formalized prior to the Revolution by the exchange of delegates between the Synod of New York and Philadelphia and the General Association of Connecticut. The Congregationalists of Connecticut had been able to complete their system with a connectional body that linked together the individual Congregational churches. This so reduced the gap which separated them from the Presbyterians (leaving only the original question of where initial jurisdiction resided in debate) that they tended to call themselves Presbyterians. This tendency to adopt the Presbyterian name was also found among the Congregationalists in Rhode Island and New Hampshire.

Following the war, the Presbyterian General Assembly of 1791 voiced its desire "to renew and strengthen every bond of union" between the Presbyterian and Congregational churches, recalling "with much satisfaction the mutual pleasure and advantage produced and received by their former intercourse." Somewhat later, when migration into central and western New York from both Pennsylvania and New England brought about an intermingling of Presbyterians and Congregationalists in a territory that had not been covered by the regional allocation, a Plan of Union was devised and adopted in 1801 which permitted the two groups to form single churches in frontier areas. "Is it wise, is it Christian," John Blair Smith, president of Union College, had asked, "to divide the sparse population holding the same faith, already scattered over the vast new territory, into two distinct ecclesiastical organizations, and thus prevent each from achieving those means of grace which both might sooner enjoy but for such division?" For more than a third of a century, the union of the two denominations was remarkably successful.

The winning of independence posed no immediate organizational problem for the Congregationalists. Their status as established churches in Massachusetts, Connecticut, and New Hampshire inhibited them from forming a connectional body that would have linked the Congregational churches across state lines. Furthermore, there was at least a strong minority among the Congregationalists which had developed an insistence upon an extreme localism in marked contrast to Lyman Beecher's conviction that "a presbytery made up of New England men, raised Congregationalists, is the nearest the Bible of anything there is." Nathaniel Emmons voiced the contrary view in 1803 when he asserted that "Association leads to Consociation; Consociation leads to Presbyterianism; Presbyterianism leads to Episcopacy; Episcopacy leads to Roman Catholicism." The resistance to any encroachment upon local rights by a higher ecclesiastical authority was especially strong among the generality of the inhabitants of the parishes who were not church members but who controlled much of the outward affairs of the state-established Congregational churches. This jealous defense of local prerogatives was less pronounced among the actual church members until the ejection of the New School synods from the Presbyterian church in 1837 rekindled old fears of ecclesiastical tyranny. The persistence and augmenting of this spirit of localism was to make it difficult for the Congregationalists to form a national organization long after their churches had been disestablished in New England.

The Presbyterian churches, since the healing of the breach between the Old Side and New Side parties in 1758, had been united in the Synod of New York and Philadelphia, and shortly after the close of hostilities a committee of the synod proposed the reorganization of the church into sixteen presbyteries, four synods, and an annual General Assembly. The "book of discipline and government," which embodied this scheme and preserved the previous right of local presbyteries to control the examination of candidates for the ministry, was approved by the synod in 1787, referred to the presbyteries for consideration, and formally adopted in 1788, with the General Assembly meeting for the first time in 1789.

The Baptists were the one major denomination that experienced significant growth during the war years, and—partly as a consequence—they were to have the greatest difficulty of all the denominations in effecting a national organization. The largest portion of the Baptists had been united in an intercolonial body, the Philadelphia Baptist Association, since 1707, but their major growth had not begun until two decades prior to the Revolution. This rapid expansion had made the initial pattern of organization unwieldy, and the process of adjustment through the formation of subsidiary associations had been interrupted by the outbreak of the war. By the time the war was over, the continued growth of the Baptists had resulted in the formation of numerous independent local associations. While these local associations maintained correspondence with one another, they had become deeply infected by the hyperindividualistic spirit of "separate" Congregationalists turned Baptist, most of whom resisted the formation of any structure which might conceivably be used to impose any degree of overhead control. As a result, proposals to effect a national organization found little support until a developing interest in foreign missions provided the occasion in 1814 for the establishment of what was intended to be a general convention of the whole denomination. Twelve years later, however, it was decided that this body should not be permitted to become anything more than a voluntary society of individuals and should be restricted in scope to the promotion of foreign missions. Thus, apart from local associations of churches, the only links which bound Baptists together were to be voluntary societies devoted to a variety of specialized interests. While this solution to their problem of national organization was to exhibit certain defects and was to create serious problems in the future, it had the immediate advantage of combining concerted action with a high degree of flexibility and local initiative.

Quakers, Episcopalians, and Methodists.—In contrast to the Congregationalists, Presbyterians, and Baptists, the Quakers suffered heavily as a result of the Revolution. Even before the war, they had lost much of their earlier dynamic, having entered a period of "quietism" and having adopted the principle of "birth-right" membership. Their refusal to countenance participation in war caused numerous defections, while those who paid war taxes or fines in lieu of military service were "disowned." Henceforth, the Quakers were to be a numerically diminishing element in American religious life, although they remained widely influential as a creative minority devoted to social reform and humanitarian service.

The greatest casualty of the American Revolution was the Church of England, which had been the church of the royal officials. This fact alone accounts for the loss of much of its popularity, but its unpopularity was vastly increased by the ardent Toryism of most of its clergy. The rector of Trinity Church in New York City reported to the Society for the Propagation of the Gospel in 1776 that "all the Society's missionaries . . . have to the utmost of their power opposed the spirit of disaffection and rebellion" in contrast to the Presbyterian clergy among whom, "after strict inquiry," he had been unable to find a single one who did not promote the Revolutionary cause. Compounding the difficulty of the Anglican churches was their dependence upon England for their ministry. Not only was it impossible to secure ordination in America, but practically all the ministers north of Maryland were missionaries drawing their support from the SPG in London. Independence cut off this source of support, since the charter of the Society limited its activities to British colonies.

Independence had other unhappy consequences for the Anglican churches. The limited supervision and co-ordination exercised by the bishop of London was brought to an end, and privileges the Anglicans formerly enjoyed as an established church were abrogated. But the most serious consequence was a large-scale depletion in the ranks of the clergy. For a time after the war, there was only one Anglican clergyman in Pennsylvania, and this was also true of North Carolina and Georgia. The others had either died or departed, and there were no new men to take their place. New Jersey was somewhat better off, with four Anglican ministers. Virginia fared best of all; but in Virginia, where before the war there had been ninety-three parishes and ninety-one clergymen, at the close of hostilities twenty-three of the parishes were extinct, thirty-four were vacant, and the remaining thirty-eight were served by only twenty-eight ministers.

In spite of this difficult situation, the few surviving Anglican clergy were successful in securing a properly consecrated episcopate and in summoning a convention in 1789 to adopt a constitution for the Protestant Episcopal Church in the United States. In conformity to the general American pattern, the new constitution provided that the laity should participate in the enactment of all ecclesiastical legislation, and it also provided that no powers should be delegated to the General Convention save those which could not be exercised by the clergy and laity in a local congregation. The newly constituted church, however, looked forward to no very hopeful future, and for several decades it had only a languishing life. In 1801, Bishop Provoost of New York laid down in discouragement his episcopal functions, being convinced that the Protestant Episcopal church would "die out with the old colonial families." Bishop Madison of Virginia and Chief Justice Marshall were equally certain that the church was too far gone to be revived. Not until well toward the middle of the nineteenth century was the Protestant Episcopal church able to make a significant recovery.

John Wesley's lay preachers had been active in the colonies during the decade preceding the Declaration of Independence, and they had succeeded in gathering about four thousand converts into their "classes." One would have guessed that the American Revolution would have had as disastrous an effect upon the Methodists as upon the generality of the Anglicans. They not only labored under the handicap of being at least nominal adherents of the Church of England, they suffered the additional disability of Wesley's staunch and articulate Toryism. Furthermore, with the exception of Francis Asbury, all the lay preachers Wesley had sent to the colonies returned to England when hostilities commenced. Asbury was determined to identify himself with the colonists and to continue his preaching, but it was no easy task. When Barratt's Chapel in Delaware was being built, an observer reflected popular sentiment when he remarked: "It's no use putting up so large a dwelling for Methodists, for after the war a corncrib will hold them all." The observer, however, was mistaken. Native lay preachers took the place of the departed English itinerants, and the Methodists, like the Baptists, continued to grow, more than tripling in number during the war years.

Wesley's break with the Church of England was precipitated by a peculiar problem of the American Methodists at the close of the American Revolution. Anglican church life in America had been so disrupted that the sacraments would no longer be available to most American Methodists unless they had an ordained clergy of their own. Wesley, therefore, responded to their need and as a presbyter consented to ordain men for what was to be the Methodist Episcopal Church. He also was prevailed upon to draft a proposed constitution for the "brethren in America," and to appoint Thomas Coke and Francis Asbury as joint superintendents of the American Methodists. Wesley somehow expected them to remain in some undefined relationship to the Church of England, but it was a wholly independent church that emerged by majority vote from the Christmas "conference" of preachers at Baltimore in 1784. Thus, the American Methodists, formed into a national body and equipped with the highly centralized circuit and conference system devised by John Wesley, were launched on an independent career that was to make them in the course of time the largest single Protestant church in America.

The "Christian" movement.—Following the American Revolution, a widespread movement developed that sought to achieve unity among Christians on the basis of the use of Bible names only, the rejection of "human" creeds, and the restriction of church usages to New Testament practice. The platform upon which those who were caught up in this movement sought to unite all denominations was expressed in the slogan: "Where the Bible speaks, we speak; where the Bible is silent, we are silent."

A group of Methodists in Virginia, led by James O'Kelley, represented the first expression of this sentiment. In the interest of unity and impressed by the stress of the revivalists upon the name "Christian" as the bond which unites, these Virginia Methodists resolved to be known by that name alone, and to adopt the Bible as their sole guide and discipline. A few years later, a Baptist in Vermont, Abner Jones, became convinced that "sectarian names and human creeds should be abandoned and that true piety alone . . . should be made the test of Christian fellowship and communion." In 1804, a Presbyterian in Kentucky, Barton W. Stone, rejected all creeds and resolved to be known by no name but "Christian." The most famous of the "Christians" or "Disciples of Christ" were Thomas and Alexander Campbell. Thomas Campbell, who was later joined by his son, formed the "Christian Association" of Washington, Pennsylvania, in 1809. The *Declaration and Address*, which was issued to announce the formation of the association, was a plea to Christians of every denomination to abandon all unscriptural doctrines and usages and to restore the original unity and purity of New Testament Christianity. While winning a significant response among many church members, the "Christian movement" failed in its objective to unite all Christians, and by the 1830's it had itself become simply another denomination.

During the whole post-Revolutionary period, the Protestant groups from the Continent, with the exception of the Dutch Reformed church, were not destined to play a large role in American religious life until their numbers had been further augmented by immigration. Even the Dutch Reformed, restricted as they were to the territory that bordered the Hudson River, made their most significant contribution as an appendage to the Congregational-Presbyterian coalition.

American Protestantism

The Protestant counteroffensive. At the close of the eighteenth century, the Protestant churches, having restored a degree of order to their respective denominational houses, were ready to embark upon a powerful counteroffensive to combat the forces of irreligion and to fashion a Protestant America. The counteroffensive was spearheaded by Congregationalists and Presbyterians and was strongly supported by Baptists and Dutch Reformed, with some aid from the Evangelical wing of the Protestant Episcopal church.

The several denominations of the coalition were firmly rooted in a common theological tradition, their church life had been largely shaped to a common pattern, and they had equipped themselves during the course of the colonial period with an understanding of the Church which permitted them to work together for the attainment of common objectives. The establishment of Brown University in 1765 serves as an early illustration of the development of a joint strategy. Scholarships for Baptist students at Harvard had been set up by Thomas Hollis at about the time Yale was being founded, and Baptist ministers were educated at practically all the colonial colleges, notably those at Philadelphia and Princeton. When Baptists had sufficient strength to establish a college of their own, the Philadelphia group which took the initiative felt restricted to two choices for its location—Rhode Island and the Carolinas—since colleges already existed in the other colonies which might have been considered. Rhode Island was chosen because it represented more nearly a mid-point among the fourteen colonies of the Atlantic seaboard. Once established, the new Baptist college proceeded to graduate twice as many Congregational as Baptist ministers during the first twenty-five years of its existence.

The Protestant America that the several denominations

sought to fashion was defined in what may roughly be described as New England terms. To suggest this is to acknowledge the obvious intellectual and theological leadership provided by the New England colleges and the closely related institution of the Presbyterians at Princeton. It also serves to call attention to the initially subordinate role in the counteroffensive that was played by the Methodists, the "Christians," and the Baptist farmer-preachers of the southern frontier. The Baptists of the middle colonies and New England as they moved west were largely an educated middle-class group, but in the rural areas of the South and on the southern frontier there was no middle class and there were few opportunities to secure an education. Consequently, outside the few urban centers of the seaboard, where Baptists had long maintained an intimate relationship with their northern colleagues and shared their interest in education, the Baptists of the South were of low social and economic status. With this differing cultural background, these Baptists developed a pattern of religious life which was disturbing to the leaders of the New England oriented counteroffensive. The "Christians," with their initial opposition to an educated ministry, to missionary societies, and to Sunday schools, were closely akin—in everything but theology—to the Baptist farmer-preachers. The Methodists were also characterized by a lack of education and an undisciplined emotionalism, for which they were viewed askance by more sober churchmen. By 1847, however, Horace Bushnell acknowledged that in the long run the Methodists could be counted as allies rather than foes. "If sometimes their demonstrations are rude and their spirit of rivalry violent," he observed, "still it is good to have such rivals for their labor is still ours; and when they have reached the state of intelligence they are after, they are sure to become effectually, if not formally, one with us. Therefore, let there be, if possible, no controversy with them; but let us rather encourage ourselves in a work so vast by the fact that we have so vast an army of helpers in the field with us." But this is to anticipate the story, and it is also to give some hint of a narrowing of Protestant concern that ultimately was to take place within the coalition.

· 5 ·

THE TASK OF THE CHURCHES DEFINED

From the very beginning, many Americans thought of themselves as a "chosen people," called of God to create in the New World a Christian society. Thus one writer began the history of Virginia with Adam and Eve in order to "show how God had so managed the past that English colonization in the present was the fulfillment of his plan." William Penn intended his domain to be a "holy experiment," designed to exhibit to the world the true character of a godly society. New Englanders were equally convinced that a unique role in God's economy had been assigned to them, being convinced that God had "sifted a whole nation" in order to plant his "choice grain" in the American wilderness. When old England "began to decline in religion," declared Edward Johnson, Christ raised "an army out of our English nation, for freeing his people from their long servitude" and created "a new England to muster up the first of his forces in." This new England, he continued, "is the place where the Lord will create a new heaven and a new earth in, new churches and a new commonwealth together."

A "holy commonwealth."—Of all the colonies, Massachusetts Bay alone was, for an extended period of time, a completely self-governing commonwealth, and it provides the best illustration of the concern to create a Christian society. Through the providence of God, so it was believed, a curious omission in the charter had given them "an open door to liberty" to fashion for themselves "a due form of government both civil and ecclesiastical." And having this freedom, they felt themselves to be under obligation to "bring into familiar and constant practice" the truths of God which at home they had been able to maintain only by profession. Thus they proposed to knit the whole body of the community together according to God's design. It was their special calling to be "a city set on a hill" to demonstrate before "the eyes of the world" what the result would be when a whole people were brought into open covenant with God.

The foundation of God's design for a "holy commonwealth" was the social covenant—a conditional contract by which God bound himself to look with favor upon a people who yielded obedience to him. Briefly stated, the basic proposition was this: "If we will have God to be our God, to pardon us and bless us; we must have him a God over us to govern us after his own will." A Christian people, if they are to enjoy the corporate blessings that God alone can bestow, must walk in his ways and fulfil his commands.

A Christian society that seeks to yield active obedience to God must operate on two levels. On the level of the community as a whole, the level of the natural man, compulsion in the form of "wholesome laws" is necessary. Since the "sins of men are like raging sea[s], which would overwhelm all if they have not banks," it is imperative that there be laws to curb the lusts of men and to restrain the overt expressions of their depravity. Such laws are to be deduced from Scripture or from nature and right reason. But, whether deduced directly from revealed precepts or merely confirmed by biblical texts, the essential test of their validity is whether or not they "really advance or tend to promote the public good." For to advance and promote the public good is to fulfil God's end in civil society and thus to honor and glorify him.

Although it is necessary to compel many and perhaps most men to heed the public good rather than their own self-interest, it was evident to the social architects of early colonial New England that God was not content with enforced obedience alone. The mark of a truly Christian society is the voluntary obedience that is given to God. "Where the Lord sets himself over a people, he frames them unto a willing and voluntary subjection unto him, that they desire nothing more than to be under his government." This was his purpose in sending Christ into the world, to turn men from "self-love" to what a later generation was to call "disinterested benevolence." When love of God and one's fellows becomes the master motive in a person's life, he becomes a willing volunteer and not a reluctant conscript in God's service.

The architects of the Bay Commonwealth were too realistic to suppose that they, as a people, would ever wholly escape from bondage to sin, and therefore they carefully devised "wholesome laws" to provide the necessary restraint and coercion. But their prayers were directed to the end that they might be granted a voluntary obedience, knowing that when "the Spirit is poured out upon a people, . . . the generality of them, or at least very many among them will be either enquiring for or walking in the way to Zion with their faces thitherward."

By the end of the seventeenth century, the leaders of the churches—even in Massachusetts Bay—were no longer in a position to dictate the wholesome laws upon which the Christian character of society in large part depended. As in the other colonies, they were forced, within the limits permitted by the government at home, to resort more and more to persuasion as a means of securing the necessary obedience to God.

A society of voluntary obedience.—Independence confronted the churches with a whole cluster of new pressures. First, it heightened their belief that the American people had a special destiny under God. The successful outcome of the Revolutionary struggle in the face of what seemed insuperable odds, they firmly believed, was a signal act of God's providence which could only be interpreted as having some greater end in view. Furthermore, with control of the new nation in American hands, the churches had a much more acute sense of direct responsibility for the proper ordering of society than they had had when ultimate control had been located abroad. This sense of responsibility was further intensified by the fact that severing the ties which had bound the colonies to the mother country also removed whatever restraining influence an established church at home had had upon government policy. Finally, the churches were compelled to think of their responsibility to the whole nation, and ultimately to the whole continent, rather than in the more restricted and hence more manageable frame of individual colonies.

Equally important was the coercion to which the churches were subjected by the American Constitution. With the winning of independence, it became a settled constitutional principle that the laws were to be determined by a majority vote of the total citizenry. This changed situation made it politically necessary, as well as spiritually desirable, to win men to voluntary obedience to the laws of God, for now all legislative action was dependent upon individual conviction and personal decision. Consequently, the moral order would be secure and the public good advanced only to the extent that a majority of the people could be persuaded to adopt the wholesome laws which God had designed for the well-being of the community. Nor was it possible to relax once these wholesome laws were enacted, for unless voluntary obedience was maintained, a political revolution at the next election could overthrow the laws and wreck all previous efforts. Thus, the churches were forced to embark on a daring venture, operating on the proposition that at least a majority of men could be persuaded to heed the public good rather than their own self-interest and become willing volunteers in God's service.

The need of the churches to operate in this fashion is inherent in the very structure of a democratic society. It has been suggested that in modern England "it is the office of Lambeth to remind Westminster of its duty to God." Lambeth, of course, is the archiepiscopal palace, and Westminster is the seat of the government. Such a statement, however, is scarcely accurate. For, in spite of the ceremonial survivals of a day long past, England is a democracy; and in a democracy the church, if it is to make its influence count, must stand by the side of every citizen, reminding him of his duty to God. In a democracy, it is the single voter in the polling booth who makes and unmakes policy. Thus in a democracy, where neither a Christian prince nor a Christian élite has the power to command, there is no substitute for a voluntary obedience to the laws of God. By no other means can the Christian faith find expression in the total life of the community.

The major responsibility of the churches in fashioning a godly society was spelled out by William Wilberforce in *A Practical View of the Prevailing Religious System* (1797). Wilberforce's intention was to provide British Christians with a practical guide to direct their endeavors into the most constructive channels, but he also spoke to American Christians. As a result of the growing role of Parliament, the problem facing British churchmen was much the same as that of their American counterparts. His *Practical View*, therefore, found a ready reception in the United States, being reprinted no less than twenty-five times on this side of the Atlantic. In his concluding appeal, Wilberforce urged the duty of all true Christians "of serving—it may be of saving—their country, not by busy interference in politics . . . , but rather by that sure and radical benefit of restoring the influence of religion." Wilberforce was not dismissing political activity as unimportant, for he himself was a busy politician directing the affairs of what has been called "the evangelical united front" and was actively engaged in securing the enactment and enforcement of godly legislation. But Wilberforce was emphasizing that, unless political efforts were undergirded by firm convictions in the minds and hearts of men, they would not avail.

The voluntary status of the churches.—The Constitution not only provided that the laws should be determined by a majority vote of the people expressing their will through their elected representatives; it also provided, with the adoption of the First Amendment, that "Congress shall make no law respecting an establishment of religion, or prohibiting the free exercise thereof." Thus there was one area of Christian concern which was to be wholly exempt from any legislative expression in the life of the nation. The churches, on the one hand, were given the right to be completely self-governing, while, on the other hand, it was insisted that they must also be completely self-supporting and self-perpetuating. They were to be dependent solely upon their own resources for their own institutional life.

Technically, to be sure, the First Amendment simply referred the establishment of religion to local option. The national government was restrained at this point, but the individual states were not. An emasculated establishment of religion—with each taxpayer assigning his rates to the church of his choice—did linger on for a generation in three of the New England states. But the principle of separation of church and state was incorporated in the constitutions of the other states, and by 1833 guarantees of full and complete religious freedom had become a part of the fundamental law of the three New England states as well. Ultimately these state guarantees were to be reinforced by an interpretation of the Fourteenth Amendment which extended the restrictions of the First Amendment to state and local governments.

The corollary of religious freedom, as has been suggested, is the voluntary church. Theologically the churches might still regard themselves as divinely constituted, but from a legal point of view they were no more than voluntary associations of private citizens. This voluntary status had revolutionary implications for the whole life and outlook of the churches which can best be seen in the long perspective of history.

Ever since the end of the fourth century, when Emperor Theodosius decreed that "all peoples which are governed by the moderation of our clemency" should become Christians, the basic assumption had been that every member of Western society was a member of the church and subject to its discipline. Thus Richard Hooker, in the sixteenth century, declared: "There is not any member of the Church of England but the same man is also a member of the commonwealth; nor any member of the commonwealth which is not also [a member] of the

Church of England." But in the United States this was no longer true. If the churches were to have any members at all, people had to be persuaded to join voluntarily. Furthermore, to win nominal members was not enough. They had to be sufficiently committed to contribute adequate financial support to the churches and to implement by voluntary action the concern of the churches to bring the will of God to bear in society.

For most of the American churches, the adoption of the principle of the separation of church and state represented no change in their status. Indeed, most of them had both sought and welcomed the establishment of the principle of full religious liberty. Only in New England was the withdrawal of ecclesiastical privileges viewed with any great alarm. But in the end, even the Congregational ministers in New England who had predicted dire evils to result from disestablishment were forced to acknowledge that the change had turned out to be a blessing in disguise.

Lyman Beecher was typical of the New England Congregationalists who clung to the conviction that state support of the churches was essential. He first reacted to disestablishment in Connecticut as if the whole church of God were about to be destroyed. He believed that the overthrow of the privileged position which the Congregational churches had inherited from colonial days would mean the triumph of irreligion and immorality, and that, as a consequence, society would rush headlong to disaster. But within a short time, Beecher had changed his mind and declared that disestablishment was "the best thing that ever happened in the state of Connecticut."

One of the things which struck Beecher most forcibly was the new feeling of solidarity which developed among Christians of all denominations as a consequence of disestablishment.

Hitherto, the "minor sects"—Baptists, Methodists, Episcopalians, Strict Congregationalists—had "complained of having to get a certificate to pay their tax where they liked" and had aligned themselves politically with the forces of "infidelity." Now, he noted with elation, the repeal of the church rates had removed "the occasion of animosity between us and the minor sects," and, as a result, "the infidels could no more make capital with them against us." Indeed, the situation was now quite the reverse. The other denominations "began themselves to feel the dangers of infidelity, and to react against it, and this laid the basis of co-operation and union of spirit." From this time forward, released from the jealousies and antagonisms engendered by a state connection, the churches of Connecticut were to display that sense of common responsibility in joint undertakings which was so largely characteristic of the Protestant churches elsewhere in the country.

Beecher's other happy discovery was that the voluntary status of the churches subjected them to "that moral coercion which makes men work." Disestablishment had "cut the churches loose from dependence on state support" and had thrown them "wholly on their own resources and God." Hitherto, he said, "our people" were content with what "our fathers had done," but now they were obliged to discard their lethargy. There were some who felt that ministers had "lost their influence," but "the fact is," asserted Beecher, "they have gained. By voluntary efforts, societies, missions, and revivals, they exert a deeper influence than they ever could" when they were accorded the special position in society symbolized by their "shoe buckles and cocked hats and gold-headed canes."

The consequence of the "moral coercion" was to transform the churches into well-organized missionary societies. No longer could they trust their special status before the law to preserve their institutional life; nor could they assume that the moral and spiritual foundations of society were secure simply because the preachers were accorded a special position in society. If the churches were to survive and make their influence felt, there was no alternative but for them to marshal all their resourcefulness and energy to win the hearts and minds of men. Beecher had not shifted his goal, which continued to be the establishment of a godly order in society, but he was forced to shift his strategy. He remained firmly wedded to the notion that God had a special destiny for America, and he remained convinced that the will of God must rule in America if America was to fulfil her destiny. But he now recognized clearly what should have been clear to him from the beginning, that in a democratic society where everything yields to the supremacy of public opinion there can be no substitute for a voluntary obedience.

"You have nothing to do but save souls."—While the churches with varying degrees of enthusiasm had accepted the necessity to rely upon voluntary means to reach their goal, most of them were too firmly rooted in the Puritan tradition to abandon the notion that the "wholesome laws" of God— other than those that dealt with specifically ecclesiastical concerns—needed to be enacted and maintained. They were needed not only to restrain the cupidity of the minority who could not be won to a voluntary obedience, but even the godly did not wholly escape the "old Adam" and, on occasion, needed to be reminded by tangible restraints of their duty to God. There was to be a growing number of Protestants in the United States, however, who would question the conviction that "wholesome laws" were indispensable to a Christian society. They minimized

the staying power of the old Adam, and believed that a sufficient number of good men would automatically create a good society. Thus, this group tended to insist that legislation and political activity were not the necessary concern of Christians as Christians. It was presumably to this segment of the Christian community that Horace Bushnell addressed himself, during the 1844 election campaign, when he said: "I cannot let politics alone until shown that politics are not under the government of God, beyond the sphere of moral obligation." Much earlier, in the midst of the campaign of 1800, John M. Mason had been disturbed by an insistence that politics is not the necessary concern of the Christian, asking rhetorically of his readers: Where did you learn the "maxim" that "religion has nothing to do with politics"?

The questioning of politics as a necessary concern of the Christian began when John Wesley's "no politics" rule was introduced into the American scene. "You have nothing to do but save souls," he told his preachers. Wesley did not regard government as beyond the sphere of God's concern, but he did regard it as beyond the concern of private men. As a staunch Tory, Wesley was fearful of the chaos that would result if the generality of men sought to exercise political responsibility. He did not intend his followers to be "republicans." Political decisions, he felt, should be left to those whom God in his wisdom had called to rule the affairs of men. In post-Revolutionary America, however, such counsel did not make much sense, for the governed were themselves the governors. In this situation, Wesley's followers had to find a new justification for his "no politics" rule and they found it in the thought of such "politicians" as Thomas Jefferson and Andrew Jackson.

Jefferson and Jackson believed in the perfectibility of man

and looked forward to the day when the need for laws would have disappeared. The laws would then be replaced within each individual by an "inner check" so that there would be no need of external restraint. The basic conviction was stated by Andrew Jackson in his inaugural address of 1829, when he said: "I believe man can be elevated; man can become more and more endowed with divinity; and as he does, he becomes more God-like in his character and capable of governing himself." The whole thrust of civilization, according to this type of thinking, was to render men more and more capable of governing them-selves. The civilized man was the virtuous man, and the virtuous man had no need for the restraint of man-made laws. Thus a natural harmony would ultimately prevail among men, and society would automatically be perfected.

Although the formula remained the same, evangelicals who obeyed Wesley's "no politics" rule sought to secure this natural harmony in a different manner. They put their confidence in the regenerated man rather than in the civilized man. The "inner check," they believed, was not the product of the diffusion of knowledge but the consequence of a conversion experience that freed the individual from bondage to sin. Thus "to convert the nation" was "to reform the nation"—a point of view articulated by Bishop McKendree when he said that "God's design in rais-ing up the preachers called Methodists in America was to reform the continent by spreading Scriptural holiness over the land." A Christian society was not one of "wholesome laws" designed to conform to the overruling government of God but a nation blessed by the harmony of converted individuals.

This "popular romanticism" was not the exclusive possession of the Methodists. The "Christians" or "Disciples of Christ," for example, were in essential agreement with the Methodist em-

73

phasis, for Alexander Campbell and Barton W. Stone had been deeply influenced both by Wesleyan ideas and by the philosophy of Lockean or Jeffersonian individualism. In the course of time, the constellation of ideas embodied in the formula of the Methodist preachers penetrated to a varying degree the thinking of all Protestant denominations. So long as the rudiments of the structured thought of a sturdy Calvinism—with its conception of the government of God finding expression in the "wholesome laws" of a Christian society—survived as a dominant current in American Protestantism, the labors of the "popular romanticists" to multiply the number of conversions served to strengthen and reinforce the activities of other Protestants who were seeking to give more explicit expression to the Protestant concern for a godly society. It was another matter, however, when the older theological structure became further eroded and the hearty optimism of nineteenth-century romanticism became dominant in the churches. The difficulty with the formula of "reforming" the nation by "converting" the nation then became apparent. The formula contained no provision for the guidance of converted individuals in discharging their political responsibilities. Indeed, it was assumed that they would be guided from within and have no need of laws. Since the redemption of all men from vice was long delayed and the promise of a natural harmony remained unrealized, the practical result of the formula in the interim was for Christians, as Christians, to neglect the fashioning of "wholesome laws." The ultimate consequence was the surrender of the concept of a Christian society. But this was some distance in the future.

In the meantime there were more pressing problems to absorb the attention of the churches.

The twin threats of "infidelity" and "barbarism."—While

the coercions inherent in a free society made it necessary for American Protestants to translate their faith into busy activity, there were two other factors which accentuated this necessity and made it doubly urgent for them to get to work. These two factors were, on the one hand, the fears aroused by the increasing popularity among important segments of the population of what was variously described as "freethinking," "infidelity," and "atheism"; and, on the other hand, the concern lest "barbarism" overwhelm the nation as a result of the removal of vast numbers of people to the frontier territory of the West where they were far removed from the civilizing and Christianizing influences of the more settled communities of the East.

Throughout the Revolutionary generation, the natural religion of the English Deists had been gaining adherents among emancipated intellectuals without creating any great stir. Indeed, evangelical Christians had even allied themselves with the rationalists in the struggle for religious liberty. This identity of interest and joint labor in a common cause had inhibited any open conflict. Furthermore, the rationalists of the Revolutionary generation tended to frown upon any widespread dissemination of their views. Although they felt personally superior to the "superstitions" of revealed religion, they believed that these foibles of the weak and the ignorant were productive of "good effects" among the masses of the people, serving to promote morality and to preserve peace and order in society. Hence they were quite ready to speak a good word for the churches and to contribute to their support as occasion demanded.

After the Revolution, the tolerant paternalism of rationalistically inclined intellectuals was replaced by the more radical views of popular pamphleteers who saw the existing churches as the great enemy of progress and who sought to win the allegiance of the masses. The competing claims of "revealed" and "natural" religion were now laid bare, and it became obvious to all that the rationalist attack was directed against the very foundation of the Christian faith. It is scarcely surprising that the leaders of the churches should have become alarmed, and it is even less surprising when it is remembered that the excesses of the later stages of the French Revolution were interpreted as a direct consequence of "infidel" thinking. Events in France, it seemed to them, had clearly demonstrated that the alternative to godliness was first anarchy and then despotism. The alarm was further compounded when many earnest churchmen were persuaded that the "deistic societies" which had been founded in several American cities were part of an international conspiracy to overthrow all religion and all government.

It was this profound sense of alarm which constituted the most immediate and most urgent summons to action and which precipitated the powerful counteroffensive of the churches.

The anxiety of the churches was also aroused by the realization that the balance of political power in the nation would ultimately shift to the West as a result of the westward movement of population. The initial reaction to the westward migration in the older communities had been a sense of relief, for it gave promise of solving some of their problems by draining off unwanted elements of the population. This was the view of Timothy Dwight:

> In a political view, their emigration is of very serious utility to the ancient settlements. All countries contain restless inhabitants; men impatient of labor; men who will contract debts without intending to pay them; who had rather talk than work; whose vanity persuades them that they are wise and prevents them from knowing that they are fools; who are delighted with innovation . . . ; who feel that every change from good order and established society will

be beneficial to themselves; who have nothing to lose, and therefore expect to be gainers by every scramble; and who, of course, spend life in disturbing others with the hope of gaining something for themselves. Under despotic governments they are awed into quiet; but in every free community they create, to a greater or less extent, continual turmoil; and have often overturned the peace, liberty, and happiness of their fellow citizens.

Dwight's was an unduly dim view of the character of those who made the long trek to the rich farmlands beyond the mountains. But whatever the character of the inhabitants it soon became apparent that a vast new empire was being carved out in the American hinterland which would ultimately have a decisive voice in determining the affairs of the nation. Lyman Beecher's *Plea for the West* was an eloquent appeal to the churches to recognize that "the religious and political destiny" of the nation would be decided in the ever multiplying frontier communities and that the urgent necessity, therefore, was to provide them with a religious ministry. Horace Bushnell's *Barbarism, the First Danger* was equally eloquent in its insistence that the great task was "to fill this great field with Christian churches and a Christian people," and that "home missions" were "the chief, the all-important work"—"the first and sublimest Christian duty which the age lays upon us."

We have the future in our charge, and we mean to see the trust faithfully fulfilled. . . . To present mankind the spectacle of . . . a religious nation, blooming in all the Christian virtues; the protector of the poor; the scourge of oppression; the dispenser of light; and the symbol to mankind of the ennobling genial power of righteous laws and a simple Christian faith—this is the charge God lays upon us; this we accept, and this by God's blessing we mean to perform.

Forced by the constitutional settlement to rely upon voluntary means to secure a voluntary obedience, the churches were compelled to marshal their full resourcefulness if infidelity and barbarism were to be successfully countered and the virtuous habits and institutions of a truly Christian society were to be firmly established. In responding to this challenge, the churches developed what were to become the typical instruments of Protestant Action in a free society where religious uniformity had disappeared and where the churches were completely on their own.

· 6 ·

THE PROTESTANT COUNTEROFFENSIVE

The churches, as we have seen, were subjected to a cluster of coercions following the winning of independence. It would be false to suggest, however, that dependence upon their own resources alone to reach the unchurched was an entirely new experience. The constitutional provisions which forced the churches to rely wholly upon voluntary means did little more than make explicit the coercion to which concerned church-men in both England and America had already been subject. In England, during the eighteenth century, the parish system had broken down owing to the movement of population from rural areas to new urban centers, while in America it had never been established with any great success. The Evangelical re-vivals had been a response to this situation in which vast numbers of people were completely unrelated to the church and knew little or nothing of the Christian faith. Evangelicalism was a theological emphasis upon the necessity for a conversion experience as the beginning point of a Christian life, while revivalism was a technique developed to induce that experience.

The situation in which the churches found themselves in

post-Revolutionary America served to strengthen the Evangelical emphasis and to reinforce their reliance upon revivalism. For, whether one thought merely of perpetuating the churches or of establishing and maintaining a godly order in society, the great need was for that clearcut commitment to the Christian faith which springs from a thoroughgoing conversion experience. It is only within this context that the subsequent strenuous efforts to promote revivals can be understood.

The technique of revivalism.—The initial reaction of ministers to the urgent need for action was a renewed emphasis upon revivalistic preaching. The crisis of decision which they sought to provoke by making their listeners vividly aware that their eternal destiny hung in the balance was now intensified by making the present danger of "infidelity" quite as repulsive and threatening as the future prospect of eternal damnation. And the present danger, as they depicted it, was equally calculated to cause the hearers to make a decision and to make it right. The words "provoke" and "calculated" and "cause," however, suggest a change in emphasis that was to become more and more pronounced.

The earliest colonial revivals had been largely unsought, being regarded as the outpouring of God's spirit upon the people—an outpouring which came in God's good time as a by-product of the faithful preaching of God's Word. "Christians," Calvin Colton remarked concerning these earlier revivals, "waited for them, as men are wont to wait for showers of rain, without even imagining that any duty was incumbent upon them as instruments." Over the course of time, however, revivals came to be regarded as evidence of "the divine blessing upon measures concerted and executed by man." Confronted by an urgent summons to action, the notion that

Christians "must wait God's time" increasingly came to be considered little more than an apology for indolence. There was not time to wait and they had no intention of doing so. To their way of thinking, "to wait God's time, in this matter, was not to wait at all." Lyman Beecher put it more bluntly when he told the clergy that they were "no longer to trust Providence and expect God will vindicate his cause while we neglect the use of appropriate means."

The means were not neglected, and the revival campaigns that stemmed from the Congregational-Presbyterian orbit stressed a doctrine of "disinterested benevolence" that had a familiar ring to American ears. John Winthrop had stated the essential point when he stood on the deck of the "Arbella" and had spoken of the "due form of government" that was to be established on the New England shore. He reminded those who had joined the "great migration" that "everyone is born in nature full of self-love, with a selfish pride that must be chastened, yet can never be expunged by natural means; but when Christ takes possession of his soul, a man conceives a great love not only to God but to his fellows." Thus in Christ one is enabled to have that "care of the public" which will "oversway all private respects."

This was the theme picked up, developed, and elaborated by such theologians of revivalism as Samuel Hopkins and Nathaniel W. Taylor as the key to Christian social responsibility. They defined sin as "selfishness," and holiness or virtue as "disinterested benevolence." The effect of conversion was to shift "the controlling preference of the mind" from a "preference for self-interest" to a "preference for disinterested benevolence." It was further insisted that true conversion, involving this shift in the preference of the mind, must express itself in action. The experience of salvation must not be interpreted as the end of the Christian life, but as its beginning. The convert, Charles G. Finney was to declare, does not escape life; he begins a new life "in the interests of God's kingdom." Working, he insisted, was quite as necessary as believing.

This emphasis upon the need to translate faith into action provided the basis for enlisting the full participation of the laity in the counteroffensive of the churches. Its practical effect was to channel the whole impulse of the religious life into active support of the highly organized system of voluntary societies. The voluntary societies, in turn, became a major instrument of the churches in their endeavor to fashion a Protestant America.

The voluntary societies.—It was to the revivals, as Lyman Beecher reported, that the churches chiefly looked "for their members and pastors, and for that power upon public opinion which retards declension, gives energy to law, and voluntary support to religious institutions." But revivalism alone, especially to the New England oriented mind of the Protestant coalition that sparked the counteroffensive, was not enough. There were, for one thing, other possible channels to the public mind—Sunday schools, cheap tracts, and religious periodicals. But more important, a whole culture was at stake— a culture that found expression in moral habits, stable institutions, and a just order in society, and that presupposed a literate people and a religious leadership that was trained in the liberal arts as well as in the Bible. Schools, academies, and colleges needed to be established, charitable causes supported, and social reforms of one sort or another fostered. Furthermore, various issues of public concern needed to be clarified, and opinion molded and sentiment mobilized in their behalf. Moreover, while the revivals supplied the churches with candidates for membership and volunteers for the ministry, the potential members and the embryo ministers needed to be instructed so that they might rightly interpret the will of God; and for this purpose Bibles, catechisms, and books were necessary in addition to provisions for formal education. Above all, ministers or missionaries needed to be sent to those "waste places" of the back country where there were no churches and consequently no leadership to initiate a revival, organize a church, or establish a school.

As early as 1796, voluntary societies began to be organized to meet such needs as these. A voluntary society was an extra-church agency, formed for a specific purpose by individuals and not related structurally to the churches. Essentially a technique for co-operative action devised by British churchmen, the voluntary society was seized upon by American Protestants as a perfect instrument by which they could pool their efforts to influence public opinion, effect reforms, meet humanitarian needs, establish colleges, provide religious instruction, organize publishing ventures, and carry on extensive and wide-ranging missionary activities.

Lyman Beecher, who was to do more than any other single individual to perfect the technique, stumbled on the usefulness of the voluntary society early in his career when, in a blaze of indignation following the slaying of Alexander Hamilton by Aaron Burr, he decided that dueling was "a great national sin" which must be eradicated. Noting that even on the floor of Congress "powder and ball" had been substituted for "deliberation and argument," he issued a call for the formation of a society dedicated to putting an end to this national disgrace. The immediate effect of the formation of the society was to arouse interest, awaken attention to the evil involved, and rally all good men to the cause.

There were several advantages to this method of procedure, not the least of which was the fact that action did not need to be delayed until a majority within a church could be persuaded to act. A few interested friends could take the initiative and then, through the society they had created, proceed to enlist broader support for the enterprise. Not only this, but voluntary societies were ideally designed to marshal the indispensable rank-and-file support behind a specific objective, and to associate "the leading minds of the laity" with the clergy in determining "what needs to be done and the means of doing it." Such associations of "working" Christians, Lyman Beecher noted, "concentrate the best hearts, the most willing hands, and the most vigorous and untiring enterprise" upon a single objective and are "eminently adapted to answer their intended purpose" of getting things done.

A still further advantage of the voluntary societies was that they provided, as British experience had made clear, a means of bypassing denominational differences in the interest of united effort. The pressing needs of the time demanded the widest possible co-operation. As the preamble to the constitution of the Philadelphia Sunday and Adult School Union was to put it: "The comparative *fewness* of Christians calls for all practicable and profitable union among themselves. *Divide* and *conquer* is the maxim of their great foe: *Unite* and *triumph* be then the motto of Christians." This the societies, defined as they were in purposive rather than creedal terms, enabled them to do. Those whose interests and convictions might otherwise be quite diverse could unite for the specific purpose for which a particular society was organized.

There were three basic types of societies: first, those that were devoted to issues of public and private morality, such as slavery, temperance, world peace, and Sabbath observance; second, those devoted to charitable causes, such as the care of orphans, the schooling of the needy, and the reclamation of "females who have deviated from the paths of virtue"; and finally, those devoted to specifically religious needs. As at a later time, within the similar structure of Catholic Action, there was an insistence that the first and great task of Catholic Action was the "religious formation" of individuals; so the primary stress of the earlier Protestant Action was upon the work of the latter group of societies. They were all parts of a single enterprise, but a solid foundation of willing obedience to the laws of God was essential to the success of them all.

The pattern of activity of the third group of societies can best be seen in the frontier communities into which they moved with a thoroughly systematized program of evangelism. The earliest missionaries dispatched by the missionary societies were itinerants. When they found a community able to provide a portion of their support, they settled down and continued their itineracy into neighboring communities as time permitted and opportunity offered. While the missionary societies were supplying the clergymen and establishing the churches, the tract and Bible societies provided the necessary literature, the Sunday School Union busied itself promoting the religious training of the children, and the education societies maintained the supply of new ministerial personnel by providing funds to aid needy theological students.

The great "Valley campaign" of 1829–31.—The fight against "infidelity" was a national concern, but it was in response to the problem of the West that a national strategy was developed.

Actually, "infidelity" did not long remain a serious threat, having been almost completely "drowned" during the three decades after 1790 in "the great tidal wave of revivalism" that swept the country, so that an English visitor in 1822–23 was able to report that "instances of openly avowed deism are rare," for "a man's reputation would be seriously injured if he were to avow himself one." The problem of reducing the multiplying communities of the West to Christian obedience, however, continued and became steadily more urgent.

The Mississippi Valley—the vast expanse of open country stretching from the Appalachians to the Rockies—was the great source of anxiety. The smallest of the states being carved out of this midland empire, it was noted, was larger than all five New England states combined, and the population of the valley was multiplying at an astonishing rate. Ohio, for example, which had only 45,000 inhabitants in 1800, had 581,000 in 1820, and ten years later 937,000 which exceeded the total of both Massachusetts and Connecticut. It was apparent that the valley would soon be able to command a majority in Congress. And the election of Andrew Jackson in 1828 demonstrated that the valley could even elevate one of its sons to the Presidency.

The initial alarm had been raised by Samuel J. Mills when he reported, following his return from a tour of inspection in 1815, that some of the valley's inhabitants had never seen a Bible or heard of Jesus Christ. It was his report more than anything else that gave impetus to the linking of local and state societies into national organizations so that they could develop and pursue a unified national strategy; the American Education Society and the American Bible Society were formed in 1816, the American Sunday School Union in 1824, the American Tract Society in 1825, and the American Home Missionary

Society in 1826—the year after the Erie Canal had opened a new gateway to the West. The circular which announced the formation of the American Home Missionary Society, declared that "a more extended effort for the promotion of 'Home Missions' is equally indispensable to the moral advancement and the political stability of the United States," and its constitution voiced the common conviction of all the societies when it asserted that "we are doing a work of patriotism, no less than that of Christianity."

Great care was exercised to preserve the interdenominational character of these societies. The publishing committee of the American Tract Society, for example, was composed of representatives of the Baptists, Congregationalists, Dutch Reformed, Episcopalians, and Presbyterians who were expected to be the "protectors" of their own respective "peculiarities," it being believed that sufficient common ground existed to load each tract with an ample measure of "divine truth." Similar safeguards secured a broad base of support in the other societies. Baptists and Episcopalians, to be sure, found it difficult to participate directly in the American Home Missionary Society because of its relationship to the establishment of churches. At this point, therefore, they tended to operate more exclusively through supplementary societies of their own. In the field, an equally harmonious spirit tended to prevail. While there was a friendly rivalry for the adherence of the converts won in the jointly sponsored revivals, strictures were largely reserved for such non-Evangelical groups as the Universalists. For a briefer time, the Methodists and their "Christian" or "Disciple" colleagues were subjects of reproach because of their undue doctrinal laxity and excessive emotionalism.

The second feature of these national societies was the close interrelationship among them. The annual meetings were held in May at the same time and at the same place, and a small group of men—through what has been called a series of "interlocking directorates"—largely controlled the policies and activities of them all. Indeed, on occasion, they even transferred funds from one society to another to meet an unusually urgent need. They do not act alone, an auxiliary society assured its members in 1826, when it reported to them the "magnificent" spectacle of the "Bible, tract, domestic missionary, Sunday school, and colonization societies" at the May meetings, "moving harmoniously on, forming so many parts of the grand whole, to the completion of that last command of our ascended Lord, 'Go and spread the influence of the gospel over every creature.'"

John Mason Peck, a Baptist missionary operating initially out of St. Louis, was responsible for initiating a great "saturation" campaign by the societies to save the valley and thus save the nation. Peck's was a remarkable vision of what the valley could become with strategically located Sunday schools, churches, colleges, and theological seminaries, and he had discovered out of his own experience a tactic that could be successfully used to increase the effectiveness of the agents in the field. He had returned to the East in 1826 to attend the General Convention of the Baptists, and he remained in New York City to present his plan to the organization meeting of the American Home Missionary Society. His principal suggestion, which received immediate approval, was that the missionaries of any one of the societies could easily act for them all, as he himself had been doing, thus multiplying their effectiveness. Each agent, as opportunity offered, could sell Bibles, distribute tracts, establish Sunday schools, organize churches, promote educational interest, and form local auxiliaries of each of the national societies, and in so doing, augment his income and solve the problem of support. The other facet of Peck's proposal was a concerted and concentrated effort to win the valley at once.

By 1828 the plans were fully developed, being given added urgency by the shift of political power that was dramatized by the impending election of Andrew Jackson to the Presidency, and in 1829 the campaign was launched. The goal of the campaign had been sketched by Lyman Beecher as early as 1816 in an address at the founding of the American Education Society. It was "a Bible for every family, a school for every district, and a pastor for every thousand souls," and Beecher proceeded to elaborate the final point which was the particular concern of the Education Society: "The prevalence of pious, intelligent, enterprising ministers through the nation, at the ratio of one for a thousand, would establish schools and academies and colleges," as well as virtuous habits; and these, in turn, "would produce a sameness of views and feelings and interests which would lay the foundation of our empire upon a rock." The only item to escape him was the Sunday school—an instrument just beginning to be developed in the year in which he spoke.

The scope of this simultaneous "saturation" campaign of the societies' valley project can be depicted adequately only by statistics. The American Bible Society proposed to supply a Bible to every family who would either buy or accept one. During the fiscal year 1829–30 23,171 Bibles were shipped into Ohio, and it was expected that the state would be completely supplied by May, 1831. Nearly as many Bibles were sent to Kentucky, more than 10,000 to Tennessee, and 14,408 to Indiana. The American Tract Society had shipped about $700 worth of tracts west of the Alleghenies in 1827, in contrast to a total of $14,927.13 for the 1829–30 fiscal year. The Sunday School Union proposed to establish a Sunday school in every place in the valley where it was practical to do so, and to do it within two years. The American Education Society busied itself organizing auxiliaries and sent Lyman Beecher to establish a theological seminary at the strategic center of Cincinnati, while the American Home Missionary Society declared that its object could not be considered accomplished until every locality was "supplied with an able and faithful minister." The multiple agency system that had been suggested by Peck was also put into operation. The 483 missionaries of the American Home Missionary Society, for example, in 1831 organized two hundred Bible classes and more than five hundred Sunday schools, reporting these achievements directly to the American Sunday School Union. The Sunday School Union, in turn, had 112 missionaries of its own (43 Congregationalists and Presbyterians, 24 Baptists, 17 Methodists, 12 Cumberland Presbyterians, 8 Episcopalians, 2 Dutch Reformed, and 6 unidentified) in the valley, and they distributed Bibles and tracts in addition to organizing Sunday schools. The activities of the interdenominational societies, of course, were supplemented by the further endeavors of the denominational societies. The Baptist General Tract Society, to cite one illustration, by 1829 had jumped its publishing to five million pages per year. It is more difficult to tell to what extent the Methodists fitted into the total operation—at what points they were co-operative and at what points competitive—but in 1828 the Methodist Book Concern distributed 3,500 Bibles, 18,000 Testaments, and 6,000 Scripture Questions.

In 1833, encouraged by the success of the valley campaign,

the societies turned their attention to the South, where ignorance seemed widespread. In many sections there was not more than one educated minister for every eight thousand square miles. In the South, however, the support enlisted was small and the results meager. There were two major reasons for this. Elsewhere the societies had depended in large part for their success upon a population heavily permeated by people of New England or Middle Atlantic background who had at least some sympathy with their general cultural objectives. An added difficulty in the South was the fact that another major current in American Protestant life—the unstructured fervor of popular Evangelicalism—was dominant. This had been a minor current at the close of the Revolution, but by 1830 the type of church life it represented was triumphant in the South, and in other parts of the nation it was beginning to outdistance the influence of the older Puritan Evangelicalism. The distinction between the North and the South at this point, of course, must not be drawn too sharply, for there were enclaves in the South that shared the cultural and religious outlook best typified by New England, and there were enclaves in the upper valley and indeed a scattered few in New England itself that were more closely related to the popular religious and cultural outlook of the South.

Farmer-preachers, circuit riders, and camp meetings.—While the churches of the Protestant coalition were busy seeking to reclaim the West through the activities of the agents and missionaries of the voluntary societies, the churches of the southern frontier—starting from scratch at the close of the Revolutionary War—were making their contribution to the general Protestant counteroffensive by developing an indigenous ministry of their own. The settlers moving westward from south of the Potomac, as a result of a differing pattern of settlement during the colonial era, were characterized by less education and culture and by more active frontier "godlessness" than was true of the westering New Englanders around the Great Lakes and in the upper reaches of the Mississippi Valley. Consequently, the Baptist farmer-preacher, the Methodist circuit rider, and the camp meeting were destined to play a much larger role among them than elsewhere.

The story of the Methodist circuit riders is familiar enough. "A Methodist preacher in those days," said Peter Cartwright, the most famous of the frontier circuit riders, "when he felt that God had called him to preach, instead of hunting up a college or Biblical institute, hunted up a hardy pony or a horse, and some traveling apparatus, and with his library always at hand, namely, Bible, Hymn Book, and Discipline, he started, and with a text that never wore out nor grew stale, he cried, 'Behold the Lamb of God, that taketh away the sin of the world.'" Cartwright had little but contempt for the young missionaries who were being sent out "to civilize and Christianize the poor heathen of the West" with, as he put it, their "manuscript sermons." On one occasion he reports that he sought to give one young missionary some good advice. "I told him to quit reading his old manuscript sermons and learn to speak extemporaneously" and that "if he did not adopt this manner of preaching the Methodists would set the whole Western world on fire before he could light his match." The people of the West, he insisted, want a preacher who can mount "a stump or a block or old log, or can stand in the bed of a wagon, and without note or manuscript, quote, expound, and apply the Word of God to the hearts and consciences of the people." Horace Bushnell was much later to make an acknowledgment, which indicated a change in his own point of view, that the Methodist preachers were "admirably adapted, as regards their mode of action, to the new west—a kind of light artillery that God has organized to pursue and overtake the fugitives that flee into the wilderness from his presence. They are prompt and effective in action, ready for all service, and omnipresent, as it were, in the field. The new settler reaches the ground to be occupied, and, by the next week, he is likely to find the circuit crossing by his door and to hear the voice of one crying in the wilderness, 'The kingdom of God is come nigh unto you.'"

The Baptists present a more complicated picture. During the first half of the nineteenth century, one-third of the Baptists were to be found in New England and New York alone, and perhaps two-thirds of all Baptists belonged within the orbit of the Protestant coalition which placed its primary reliance upon missionary activities carried out through voluntary societies. The Baptist churches, to be sure, were multiplying so rapidly that they had to utilize in the ministry many men of limited formal education. Their zeal in founding academies and colleges, however, is ample testimony that they never lost sight of the ideal of an educated ministry.

But there was another current in Baptist life which stemmed from the "Separate" Baptists who established themselves on the early frontier of the Piedmont region of the South, where educational opportunities were sparse and financial resources meager. It was from this area that self-supporting farmer-preachers moved over the mountains with the initial wave of westward migration. Of these men, Theodore Roosevelt remarked in *The Winning of the West:* "They lived and worked exactly as did their flocks . . . ; they cleared the ground, split rails, planted corn, and raised hogs on equal terms with their parishioners." And the churches they formed waited for no help from missionaries sent to them by missionary societies but proceeded to "raise up" additional preachers out of their own number to evangelize neighboring communities.

The reliance of these Baptists upon the untutored farmer-preacher, which initially had been the product of necessity as well as a reflection of their cultural milieu, hardened into a matter of principle when the two streams of Baptist migration mingled along the Ohio River and its tributaries. To hear the reports of the missionaries, John Taylor commented, "it would seem as if the whole country was almost a blank as to religion" and that there was not one preacher in the whole area who deserved the name until they arrived, but "it is probable that these men think that but few deserve the name of preachers but missionaries." Daniel Parker, another early farmer-preacher was equally disdainful, pointing out that God did not send Jonah to Ninevah through a missionary society, nor was he "sent to a seminary of learning to prepare him to preach to these Gentiles; but was under the tuition of a special order of God, and was in no case under the direction of any body of men whatever, neither did he look back to a society formed to raise money for his support." These Baptists, with their opposition to an educated ministry and to all forms of organized missionary endeavor, were a strange amalgam of a highly traditional Calvinist theology and a highly uncritical appropriation of an extreme form of Jacksonian individualism. While as an organized group they never were to constitute a majority of the Baptists on the southern frontier, their thinking deeply influenced the whole Baptist ethos of the region.

The Presbyterians on the southern frontier did not wholly

escape pressure to lower their educational standards for the ministry. For them the pressure arose out of the great "camp meeting" revival that began around 1800. Confronted by an acute shortage of ministers, Presbyterians in eastern Kentucky and Tennessee began ordaining men who did not meet the educational standards of the denomination. This led to a schism in 1809 which resulted in the formation of the Cumberland Presbyterian Church. The revival was also to be the occasion for a larger defection of Presbyterians into the ranks of the "Christians."

The "Christians" or "Disciples of Christ" associated with the leadership of Alexander Campbell and Barton W. Stone were confined almost entirely to the Ohio Valley and represented what was perhaps the most typical as well as one of the most vigorous and influential forms of Protestantism on the southern frontier. This "brotherhood" of locally organized churches, as has previously been noted, was the product of a desire to unite all Christians by dropping all party names and all human creeds and by taking their stance on the Bible alone. Theologically, they were strongly Wesleyan, as was made transparently clear when Stone and his colleagues were put on trial by the Presbyterians as a result of their doctrinal and ecclesiastical laxity at the great Cane Ridge camp meeting. Philosophically, Campbell had been deeply influenced by the writings of John Locke before he left Scotland and the whole movement exhibited a hyperindividualistic spirit. Ecclesiastically, their churches betrayed many affinities with the Baptists with whom Campbell had been associated for a number of years following his break with the Presbyterians. Furthermore, Campbell did more than any other single person to generate an opposition to missionary societies and a theologically educated ministry.

Augustus Longstreet, in his study of the Georgia frontier, has remarked that "the honest Georgian preferred his whiskey straight and his politics and religion red hot." So it was on much of the southern frontier, where life was often raw, rough, and uncontrolled. Here physical manifestations of religious excitement, which tended to be frowned upon in Yankee areas, were permitted and sometimes encouraged. The camp meetings, great outdoor gatherings for preaching which lasted several days, was the major evangelistic device in the years following 1800. Initiated by the Presbyterians when they began to hold sacramental meetings under the trees, they were later repudiated by them because of their noise, confusion, and uninhibited "exercises." Later the camp meeting was domesticated by the Methodists and became a characteristic Methodist technique for enlisting group pressure to induce conversions.

These several denominations on the southern frontier constituted the second force in the Protestant counteroffensive. Their achievements, measured by the genuine piety awakened and the moral order introduced as well as by the increase in church membership, were more significant than their cultural idiosyncrasies. In balancing the account, it must be remembered that the southern frontier was "crude, turbulent, and godless," and it is unlikely that anything other than this popular form of Protestant Evangelicalism could have tamed it.

The two-pronged counteroffensive of the churches had demonstrated by the middle of the nineteenth century that, with persuasive power alone, the churches "could 'Christianize' the nation—set the accepted mores and moral patterns, and provide the foundation of commonly shared religious beliefs which were so essential for the being and well-being of the Republic." Protestant church membership had increased tenfold in the fifty years from 1800 to 1850. The statistics are somewhat uncertain, but it has been estimated that in 1800 one person out of every fifteen was a member of a Protestant church; in 1835 one out of eight; and in 1850 one out of every seven. When it is remembered that church attendance among several of the denominations was frequently three times the membership and that the constituency of a church was often computed as twice the number of attendants on a given Sunday, the magnitude of the achievement becomes more apparent. Even though "the flame of religious zeal burned with significant brightness only in the hearts of a minority," the life of the whole community was deeply penetrated by the basic attitudes inculcated by the churches, and the churches standing beside the courthouse on the village square became symbols of the common conviction that morals and good order rested upon religion. Thus "the church building, the services within it, and all the self-denying Sabbath customs were symbolic expressions of a folk belief in an eternal and changeless moral order upon which society rests." The universal esteem in which the churches were held was a measure of the extent to which they had effectively penetrated the life of society.

· 7 ·

THE REALIGNMENT OF
AMERICAN PROTESTANTISM

The first half of the nineteenth century witnessed a realignment in the relative numerical strength of the Protestant denominations and brought to an end most of the surviving elements of the Puritan age. During these years, Puritan Evangelicalism was giving way to popular Evangelicalism, and for the rest of the century American Protestantism was to be defined almost wholly in Methodist terms. The final decade and a half prior to mid-century also witnessed the development of severe strains within the several denominations and the temporary collapse of the united efforts of the Protestant coalition.

The reshuffling of the denominations.—Church statistics are never wholly accurate, being compiled with varying degrees of care and subject to varying interpretations, since some churches report the total baptized membership while others include only adult communicants. Moreover, as an indication of relative denominational strength they are subject to some distortion by varying requirements for membership, with some groups having a much higher proportion of largely nominal members. These uncertainties, however, are not sufficient to obscure the marked shift in numerical rank among the several denominations that had taken place by 1850.

At the end of the colonial period, the Congregationalists and the Presbyterians had been the two largest denominations; by 1850 they had both been supplanted by the Methodists and the Baptists. Statistically, the Methodists were far in the lead with a reported membership of 1,324,000. The Baptists followed with 815,000 members. The Presbyterians were third with 487,000; while the Congregationalists, who had formerly headed the list, were fourth with 197,000. The Lutherans, profiting by a recent surge of immigration, were fifth with 163,000; and the Disciples, a new entrant on the American religious scene, were sixth with 118,000 members. The Episcopalians, having made a vigorous recovery from the low ebb they experienced for more than a generation after independence, were in seventh place with 90,000 adherents.

These membership figures, of course, are not comparable to twentieth-century membership statistics which are inflated by the practice of including many who have only the most nominal relationship to a church. A closer approximation to modern figures is provided by an analysis made by the American Education Society in 1830. This analysis sought to arrive at the more comparable "church population" or "constituency" of each denomination by giving due weight to differing denominational definitions of membership and by estimating the total group related in one way or another to a particular denomination. The results for 1830 were as follows: Calvinist Baptists, 2,743,453; Methodists, 2,600,000; Presbyterians, 1,800,-000; Congregationalists, 1,260,000; Episcopalians, 240,000. While these inflated figures gave added comfort to all denominations, they still left the Methodists and Baptists far in the lead. What they do indicate is that, while there was a marked redistribution of denominational strength in the early decades of the nineteenth century, there does not seem to have been—with the exception of the Lutherans and the Disciples—any significant change in numerical rank since 1830.

The conventional explanation of the earlier shift in denominational strength is that the size of the several denominations was determined by their relative effectiveness in meeting the religious needs of the western frontier. This would seem to be only partially true, for the Baptists made equally striking gains elsewhere and Methodist growth was not restricted to the frontier communities. The Baptists reaped a large harvest from the disaffection created within New England Congregationalism by the "liberalizing" tendencies which were to culminate in the Unitarian explosion of 1815–20, and an age which emphasized the supreme and literal authority of the Scriptures found plausibility in the Baptist insistence upon believers' baptism. Methodist zeal and enthusiasm, in turn, was calculated to win a response among many people along the seaboard as well as on the frontier. The partial truth of the frontier explanation is the fact that in a time when the population is rapidly expanding, those churches profit most which are able to supply enough ministers to take advantage of the opportunities offered to gather new churches. This both the Methodists and the Baptists were able to do—in the burgeoning mill towns of the East as well as on the frontier.

The triumph of popular Evangelicalism.—The distinction between two strands of Evangelicalism in American Protestant life has been mentioned repeatedly. The one was characterized by the emphases which found expression in the coalition effected by those denominations with a relatively strong Puritan or Calvinistic heritage; the other was characterized by the emphases which found most conspicuous expression among the Methodists. During the 1830's this distinction began to be obliterated, and by 1850 Evangelical Protestantism had become defined almost wholly in Methodist terms.

Popular Evangelicalism, of course, tended to become more sober with the passing of time and tended to lose many of its cultural antipathies. After 1830, for example, the Methodists began to establish colleges. This activity, to be sure, was accompanied by some reservations. The statement of 1834 which proposed the founding of DePauw University contained the assurance that the Indiana Conference was "aware that when a Conference Seminary is named, some of our preachers and many of our people suppose we are about to establish a manufactory of which preachers are to be made, but nothing is farther from our views." In spite of such assurances, within five years what was to become the Boston University School of Theology was specifically established to provide theological education. Even Alexander Campbell in 1840 was to found Bethany College and spend the remaining years of his life as a college president.

Much more significant than the tendency of the "Methodist" groups—which included the "Christians" or Disciples, Free Will Baptists, United Brethren, and the Evangelical Church as well as the Methodists themselves—to become more sober and culturally respectable, was the reverse tendency which expressed itself in the rapid shift of other denominations into the Methodist camp.

To the extent that Methodism possessed a theological interest, its most distinctive features were a frank acceptance of the doctrine of free will and the affirmation of a doctrine of Christian "perfection." Even more significant was the distinction involved in the relative importance attached to sound doctrine. Evangelicalism in general stressed the primacy of heart religion manifesting itself in the conversion experience, but the churches which stood most directly within the Calvinist tradition had not forgotten the importance of sound doctrine and—in a subordinate way—of proper church order. Methodism, on the other hand, stressed an understanding of the Christian life which emphasized the conversion experience and individualistic morals almost to the exclusion of any doctrinal interest, and it tended to think of Christianity as an evangelistic movement which had few implications for any proper church order. It was not inclined to make more than the barest minimum doctrinal affirmation a test of fellowship and felt some hesitancy in allowing even basic theological differences to stand in the way of co-operation with those who seemed to be of like heart.

Furthermore, the sense of responsibility for society in any direct sense sat rather lightly upon the Methodists. They gave little attention, as we have seen, to the necessity for "wholesome laws" and tended to equate converting the nation with reforming the nation, believing—in the words of a Methodist historian—that "if the man's soul was saved fundamental social change would inevitably follow." In practical terms, since Methodists as citizens could not avoid adopting some position on political and social issues, this meant that they were apt either to indorse any current reform that seemed to be "good," or, with equal alacrity, to defend any social order that did not interfere with their evangelistic activities.

The shift in the old-line churches from a Puritan Evangelicalism to a popular Evangelicalism can best be seen in Charles G. Finney, whose revivals swept central and western New York from 1825 to 1835 and who preached his way in Presbyterian and Congregational pulpits to a full-blown Methodism. A lawyer who had received "a retainer from the Lord Jesus Christ to plead his cause," Finney began his evangelistic activity with the conservative Evangelical views of his theological mentor, George W. Gale, but he rapidly moved into the orbit of the New Haven theology of Lyman Beecher and Nathaniel W. Taylor. In the hands of these men, traditional Calvinism had been modified almost beyond recognition on the point of "free will" by an involved restatement designed to provide an effective basis for their revivalistic efforts.

Finney was much less subtle than his Congregational and Presbyterian colleagues and tended to state bluntly what many of them were thinking. "There is a sense in which conversion is the work of God," he admitted. But there is also "a sense in which it is the effect of truths" and "a sense in which the

101

preacher does it," and "it is also the appropriate work of the sinner himself." The actual turning to God, he explained with an emphasis that suggested that a person saves himself through choice, is the work of the individual. It is what God requires of the individual, and what God requires of him must be something that God cannot do for him. "It must be your voluntary act." Nor was Finney one to dwell unduly on theological distinctions. When the Presbyterians began to be agitated by theological controversy, Finney said that "their contentions and janglings are so ridiculous . . . that no doubt there is a jubilee in hell every year about the time of the meeting of the General Assembly." It is true that he would tell a Universalist that he had no more religion than his horse, but, at the same time, he would warn his converts not "to dwell on sectarian distinctions, or to be sticklish about sectarian points." After 1835, when he began dividing his time between a pastorate in New York City and a professorship at Oberlin, Finney adopted the Wesleyan view of "Christian perfection," becoming largely responsible for the marked emphasis upon "holiness" and "the higher Christian life" in the "prayer meeting" revivals of 1857–59.

Finney's work was supplemented by a host of itinerant evangelists, some of whom were imitators with little formal education and some of whom were his own converts who had been trained at the Institute of Practical Education at Whitesboro, New York, or at Oberlin. Even the more culturally respectable New Divinity men among the Congregationalists, Presbyterians, and Baptists tended to move into his camp. Lyman Beecher, distressed by Finney's bluntness and unconventional procedures, had said that if Finney ever entered New England, he would meet him at the border and fight him all the way to Boston, but in the end it was Beecher who invited Finney to come to Boston. Horace Bushnell, who is often regarded as an enemy of revivals, not only defended them but came to recognize, while deploring "artificial" fireworks, that there was need for some excitement to attract the attention of the unconverted and effect a change in them.

Bushnell also provides evidence of the redefinition of the churches' responsibility for society in essentially Methodist terms, for he could speak on occasion of "a nation of free men, self-governed, governed by simple law without soldiers or police." Rufus Anderson, secretary of the American Board of Commissioners for Foreign Missions—the old foreign mission bastion of the voluntary society complex—supplies equally convincing testimony to the change that was taking place. In 1845 he insisted that the responsibility of the churches did not extend beyond an individualistic winning of converts one by one to the cause of Christ. "That point being gained," he said, "and the principle of obedience implanted, and a highly spiritual religion introduced, social renovation will be sure to follow." Explicitly rejected as an objective of missions was the "reorganizing, by various direct means, of the structure of that social system of which the converts form a part." This notion of automatic social renovation caused even the churchmen of the old-line denominations to regard revivals as possessing a certain sacramental quality in the life of a community, being outward evidence of an inward desire to sanctify the whole community to God, and indeed did so. Thus Albert Barnes, minister of the First Presbyterian Church of Philadelphia, could state that there is seldom "a city or town or peaceful hamlet that has not been hallowed by revivals of religion; and in this fact we mark the evidence, at once, that a God of mercy presides over the destinies of this people."

Around 1830 many Presbyterians began to resist the sweeping tide of popular Evangelicalism with a sturdy defense of the traditional standards of doctrine and church order, only to find that they had divided the church and subjected themselves to ridicule and abuse. Even the Lutherans, with their confessionalism undercut by pietism, were brought temporarily into this main current of American Protestantism, while the Unitarians, much to Lyman Beecher's amazement, made an abortive attempt to hold revivals of their own.

The strains of controversy.—Tension within American Protestantism became acute after 1830. But a shattering explosion within Congregationalism had occurred somewhat earlier.

Even before independence had been won, the Congregational ministers of eastern Massachusetts, under the influence of Jonathan Mayhew and Charles Chauncy, had been divided into a liberal and an orthodox party. They lived together in an uneasy truce, with the liberals disguising their unitarian and universalist convictions until the election of a liberal to the Hollis Professorship of Divinity at Harvard in 1805 provoked the founding of Andover Theological Seminary in 1808 by the orthodox. The issue was not fully joined, however, until 1815, when the true sentiments of the liberals were revealed in a pamphlet which reprinted some of their correspondence with English Unitarians. A division was immediately precipitated, with about one hundred churches in Massachusetts and a scattered few elsewhere joining the Unitarian faction. The Unitarians made little effort to propagate their views, being convinced that cultural advance would ultimately lead others to join them and, in the meantime, being quite content, as someone has said, to maintain their private faith in "the fatherhood of God, the brotherhood of man, and the neighborhood of Boston."

Views similar to those of the Unitarians were held by the Universalists, a lower-class group stemming from the evangelistic activities of John Murray in eastern Massachusetts during the late eighteenth century. Actively propagandist, the Universalists moved into the newer communities of the West, where for a time they were a major religious force and where they exerted a far greater direct influence than the Unitarians —if only by way of reaction—upon the developing theology and institutional patterns of American Protestantism. After 1840, however, the Universalists had begun a sharp and steady decline—a decline that was probably hastened by their encounter with Spiritualism.

More serious in its ultimate consequences than the Unitarian-Universalist defection was the controversy during the 1830's which dramatized the tension between the forces of Puritan and popular Evangelicalism and led to an Old School–New School division among both the Presbyterians and the Baptists. Men in both denominations were disturbed by the growing influence of the New Divinity of Yale, as formulated by Nathaniel W. Taylor and popularized by Beecher and Finney. It seemed to them to represent not only an undermining of some of the cardinal doctrines of the Christian faith but also a developing laxity of ecclesiastical practice that in the end would make impossible any attempt to maintain sound doctrine. While there were other factors in the controversy, this was the main issue, and it transformed such a person as Ashbel Green, who had hitherto been an eager participant in the Protestant coalition, into an earnest advocate of traditional Presbyterian views.

Among the Presbyterians, the controversy was initiated with charges of heresy lodged against Albert Barnes and Lyman Beecher. Both cases were ultimately brought before the General Assembly in 1836; a New School majority dismissed the charges against Barnes, whereupon the charges against Beecher were withdrawn. The latter move was no more than a strategic retreat by the Old School party to permit them to return to the "hustings" to marshal further support. The following year, the Old School party commanded a clear majority in the General Assembly and proceeded to expel the predominantly New School synods from the church, thus leaving them no alternative but to form a separate New School Presbyterian Church. The Old School victory, in the end, was not to be complete, for the two factions were reunited during and immediately after the Civil War, reintroducing thereby the New School leaven. Furthermore, the fact that Albert Barnes's eleven-volume commentary on the Bible, published between 1832 and 1853, sold over a million copies was adequate testimony to his continuing influence.

Among the Baptists, the defenders of the traditional standards constituted a large and significant bloc, especially in the back-country areas of both the East and the West. When this group failed to capture the denominational machinery, a defection occurred during the early 1830's which carried with it many local associations. These churches and associations, however, adopted such a rigidly defensive posture that they could do little more than eke out a dwindling existence, and their withdrawal left the other Baptist churches open to what had now become the dominant current of popular Evangelicalism.

Problems of varying seriousness for the different denominations were created during the 1830's and 1840's by the rise of Mormonism, the millenarian excitement generated by the Millerites, the interest in Spiritualism aroused by "the Rochester rappings" of the Fox sisters, and the dissension occasioned by the development of anti-Masonic sentiment. But the major disruptive influence, which became acute in the 1840's, was the emotion generated by the slavery controversy. The Methodists and Baptists were divided into separate bodies by this issue in 1844 and 1845, and the New School Presbyterians underwent similar division in 1857. The Old School Presbyterians and the Episcopalians avoided disruption at this point by remaining aloof to the whole controversy, while the Disciples of Christ were too loosely associated to be divided. In 1861, after the outbreak of hostilities, the southern Old School Presbyterians formed the Presbyterian Church in the Confederate States of America, and in 1864 the southern New School synod united with them. The reunion of the northern Old School and New School churches took place in 1869. The division between the North and the South among the Presbyterians, however, has persisted, as it has among the Baptists; and it was not until 1940 that the Methodists were reunited.

The collapse of the Protestant coalition.—The late 1830's marked the beginning of the collapse of the complex of voluntary societies through which the Protestant coalition had operated so effectively. The major factor in the collapse was undoubtedly the lessening sense of urgency for combined effort once the threat of "infidelity" was overcome and the problem of "churching" the West was reduced to manageable proportions. The establishment of what seemed to be a stable, churchgoing society defined in Protestant terms made it possible for the churches to turn their attention more and more to denominational concerns and permitted them to devote more of their energies to purposes of denominational aggrandizement. The precipitating factor in the collapse of the coalition, however, was the Old School–New School controversy.

In 1837 a group of Old School Presbyterians gained control of the Presbyterian General Assembly. Frightened by the "liberal" or "Arminian" tendencies of the New Divinity of Yale, the Old School group expelled the New School synods. At the same time the Plan of Union with the Congregationalists was abrogated, and further participation in the American Home Missionary Society, the American Education Society, and the American Board of Commissioners for Foreign Missions was prohibited. These arbitrary actions, in turn, provoked the development of a stiff-necked Congregationalism which viewed the whole Presbyterian system of church government as an instrument of tyranny. This sentiment put an end even to any continued operation of the Plan of Union with the New School Presbyterians long before it was formally repudiated by the Congregationalists in 1852. Henceforth the Congregationalists were to be so overwhelmingly dominant in the three societies from which the Old School Presbyterians had withdrawn that they lost their interdenominational character and became simply agencies of the Congregational churches.

The Baptists and the Episcopalians had largely limited their direct participation in the Protestant coalition to the activities carried on by the American Bible Society, the American Tract Society, and the American Sunday School Union. This participation was now to be reduced by the growing influence of the "high church" views of Bishop J. H. Hobart among the Episcopalians and by a developing "high church" sectarianism among the Baptists which found its most extreme expression in the old Southwest. Baptist participation, of course, had also been reduced by the Old School defection, and Baptist sentiment was to be further exacerbated by an action of the American Bible Society in 1836. The Bible Society in that year abandoned the precedent established in the Burmese translation of the Scriptures and refused to permit Baptist missionaries in India to translate the Greek word *baptizo* clearly to indicate immersion instead of merely transliterating it. The result of this action was a Baptist withdrawal and the establishment by the Baptists of the American and Foreign Bible Society. The other societies of both the Episcopalians and the Baptists, which hitherto had been regarded as largely supplementary in their operations, now tended to become more frankly competitive.

The collapse of the coalition, however, was only temporary. The triumph of popular Evangelicalism in the major denominations provided a new bond of unity and the pressing problems of the burgeoning cities after the Civil War were to create a new demand for united action. It was within this context that the coalition was to be renewed with the Methodists as full partners.

· 8 ·

A PROTESTANT AMERICA

Protestantism had been the dominant religious and cultural force in the United States from the beginning, but by the middle of the nineteenth century it had established undisputed sway over almost all aspects of the national life. It was a Protestant America that had been fashioned by the churches; and the influence of the churches, as has been suggested in an earlier chapter, extended far beyond their somewhat narrowly defined membership. The vast majority of Americans, even when not actual communicants, regarded themselves as "adherents" of one church or another; and among the populace at large the patterns of belief and conduct—both private and public, individual and corporate—were set by the churches.

This dominance of the culture can be documented in many ways. The American democratic faith, for example, was grounded during these years in "a frank supernaturalism," being based on Christian ideas as understood and interpreted by Protestants. Documentation can also be found in the fact that, during the middle decades of the century, the religious press was growing more rapidly than the secular press both in number of periodicals and circulation. Whitney R. Cross, in his study of central and western New York, discovered how widely and avidly these religious journals were read, and he found it difficult to understand how they could have had such a widespread appeal. After weighing several indirect explanations of their attraction, he was forced to conclude that the "inescapable" fact seems to be that even "laymen read and relished the theological treatises" they contained. The power and prestige of Protestantism is further attested by the public response to the revivals that swept the urban centers on the eve of the Civil War. It was noted that "there was remarkable unanimity of approval among religious and secular observers alike, with scarcely a critical voice heard anywhere." Robert T. Handy suggests that "the cultural dominance of Protestantism" can also be seen in the ease of transition to a public tax-supported school system—the transition being "palatable to Protestants because the schools were rather clearly Protestant in orientation." This cultural dominance was equally apparent in higher education, as an observer in 1857 reported: "We might go through the whole list of American colleges and show that, with here and there an exception, they were founded by religious men and with mainly an eye to the interests of the church." This was the America the churches sought to maintain as they confronted the new problems of the post–Civil War years.

In spite of the tensions which had developed during the 1830's and 1840's, the churches themselves were surprisingly homogeneous and self-confident. The war was over and, while the South was beset with the problems of Reconstruction, the economy of the rest of the country was booming. The tensions which had divided some of the denominations had been submerged in the sweeping advance of popular Evangelicalism, and all the denominations had become remarkably similar in character and outlook. Nor did the churches see any reason to suppose that they would not continue to grow and their influence to increase. There were problems, to be sure, but however urgent they might become, past success fostered the conviction that they would not prove insurmountable.

The primary effect of the new problems was to force the churches to shift their focus. Whereas their great challenge prior to the Civil War had been to evangelize a westward-moving population, the great task during the decades that followed the war was to win and to hold the vast tide of people flowing into the cities. A large-scale redistribution of population had been taking place as people from hilltop villages and back-country farms moved first to the new mill towns in the valleys and then to the larger commercial and industrial centers, where an increasing number of people from abroad were also to be found. Thus the churches were faced with the necessity of duplicating among the new urban populations the success they had had among those who had created a farm and village civilization behind the receding frontier.

The urban counteroffensive.—The churches did not long delay the initiation of a counteroffensive to meet the problems arising from the new migration to the cities. The Finney revivals had been directed more and more to this end, as were those of Dwight L. Moody later in the century. City mission societies had begun to be organized as early as 1816. Initially they were preoccupied with distributing tracts and Bibles; later they assumed several different forms—"rescue" missions, seamen's institutes, and "church extension" agencies. The great instrument of the urban counteroffensive of the churches, however, was to be the Young Men's Christian Association.

At the outset, the major flow of population into the cities came from the farms and villages where the churches had been most effective in shaping the life of the total community. The move to the cities, however, tended to relax the subtle coercion of habit and emotional association as well as community pressure which had served to bind these people to their church at home. The inevitable result was a weakening of religious and moral ties, with many of the transplanted Christians tending to "backslide" in the urban environment. In this population movement, young men in their teens—striking out on their own for the first time—formed an important segment.

The Young Men's Christian Association was formed with these young men in mind, seeking to reach them as soon as they arrived in the city and to hold or win them for the Christian faith. Like so many of the other instruments of Protestant

Action, the Y.M.C.A. was a British importation, the first association having been organized in England in 1844 by a "dozen youthful salesmen in a London dry goods store." Seven years later the movement had spread to the United States, where its success was almost instantaneous, with 205 local Y.M.C.A.'s having been formed by 1860. The Boston Y.M.C.A. was the earliest of the American associations. It described itself as "a social organization of those in whom the love of Christ has produced love to men; who shall meet the young stranger as he enters our city, take him by the hand, direct him to a boarding house where he may find a quiet home pervaded with Christian influences, introduce him to the church and Sabbath school, bring him to the Rooms of the Association, and in every way throw around him good influences, so that he may feel that he is not a stranger, but that noble and Christian spirits care for his soul." Prayer meetings, Bible classes, a reading room, an employment bureau, and a lodginghouse register were the principal features of the program.

The Y.M.C.A. claimed to be "a mission of the evangelical churches to young men," but the eager and ardent youth of the "Y" were not content to restrict their Christian witness to other young men. They conceived the whole community as their mission. They collected funds to aid the destitute, cared for the sick in hotels and lodginghouses, and conducted "ragged schools" for the children of the poor. They engaged also in evangelistic activity—working in rescue missions, distributing tracts, and going out "to preach on street corners, at the wharves, in neighborhood fire houses—wherever they could gather an audience." Called "the flying artillery of Zion," these young men became a sturdy arm of the churches, charged with preaching the gospel to the unchurched of the cities. These associations, declared a speaker in 1859, constitute a "light-armed, chosen, consecrated, fleet of foot, and trusty band sent out to reconnoiter and open the way for salvation to follow."

The Y.M.C.A.'s also assumed leadership in initiating and promoting community-wide revival campaigns. The great "prayer meeting" or "businessmen's" revival of 1857–59 grew out of the noonday prayer meetings of the New York Y.M.C.A. and was carried forward by other associations in the major cities. Through his connection with the Chicago Y.M.C.A., Dwight L. Moody was introduced to organized evangelistic work and induced to forsake his business activities and devote himself wholly to conducting revival campaigns, and he quickly became the single most influential person in the entire Y.M.C.A. movement. A reciprocal relationship developed between Moody and the Y.M.C.A. As the most immediately available interdenominational agency at the local level, the Y.M.C.A. provided the necessary community-wide co-ordination for his campaigns; while he, in turn, was always available to raise funds to support the expanding work of the "Y." In addition he was the key figure in the success of the Student Christian Movement on the college campuses.

The ordinary activities of the churches and the extraordinary activities of rescue missions and the Y.M.C.A. were successful in seeking out and reaching many of the new urban inhabitants, but these efforts were not particularly systematic. After the Civil War, the Y.M.C.A.'s had transformed the United States Christian Commission—which they had organized as the wartime instrument of the churches for ministering to the soldiers—into the American Christian Commission to serve as a board of strategy for the churches in dealing with the urban problem. It was at a meeting of the American Christian Commission in 1868 that a speaker pointed to the "startling fact" that the gospel was not being "presented to every creature." Many individuals and whole families were being missed. The great need was for the churches to reach out in systematic fashion to every home. To accomplish this and to keep in touch with people during their frequent moves within the cities, a monthly house-to-house visitation was proposed.

There were scattered efforts to carry out such a systematic visitation program, but the problem was larger than any one church or denomination could solve. It was not until the American branch of the Evangelical Alliance, organized in 1867, adopted the proposal as a central feature of its program that a large-scale visitation was attempted. Josiah Strong was the leader of the Alliance, and he was convinced a community-wide, house-to-house visitation could provide the "personal, living, love-convincing touch" that was needed between the churchgoer and the non-churchgoer:

> Christians must go to the multitude, must search them out in the workshop and the home, . . . must go not once as a census taker, but repeatedly, to establish friendly relations, to acquire a personal influence, to study the temporal and spiritual needs of the family and do all possible good.

The co-operation of the churches in such regular visitation, he declared, will "do much to neutralize the evil effects of constant moving," for in this way "the family is followed with Christian influence and found by another visitor, who helps to reunite church ties." By 1889, as a result of the Alliance's efforts, "a systematic and continuous watch-care over every part of the community" had been started in forty cities.

Those from the hinterland accounted for only a part of the population flowing into the cities. The other part came from abroad, and the mounting tide of new Americans presented the churches with a much more difficult problem. The older Americans as they came into the cities brought with them memories of religious emotions which needed only to be rekindled. The immigrants from abroad, however, came from widely differing religious traditions, and they were isolated from the existing churches as well as from the community at large by language and cultural barriers.

The first requirement in an approach to the immigrant groups was a ministry in their own language, and this the churches sought to provide as soon as any particular nationality group began to arrive in significant numbers. Thus Baptists, who were ultimately to carry on a ministry to twenty-one different nationality groups in as many different languages, began work among the Germans in 1846, the Scandinavians in 1848, the French Canadians in 1853, the Poles and Portuguese in 1888, and the Italians in 1894. Congregationalists, Presbyterians, and Methodists developed a ministry among the same foreign-language elements in the population, and among the Bohemians, Hungarians, Slovaks, Rumanians, and Russians as well. The recruiting of a "native ministry" was difficult at first, but as an increasing number of converts were secured training institutes were organized and most seminaries assumed responsibility by establishing a foreign-language department for a specific nationality group. By the end of the century, trained personnel had been supplied in such numbers that it became necessary to make urgent appeals for funds to put them to work.

Local churches carried on much of the missionary activity among the immigrant groups through home visitation and the employment of specialized personnel to conduct Sunday school classes and worship services. In other instances, mission centers were established which soon developed into foreign-language churches. In time these churches tended to become bilingual and ultimately many of them were assimilated into the existing denominational structure of Protestantism as English-speaking churches. A still greater number of these churches, within two or three generations, were left to dwindle and die as their members completed the process of adjustment to American life and found a place for themselves in the older churches.

Another imaginative response to the urban situation was the "institutional" church. Churches in growing metropolitan areas have always been plagued by the fact that people do not "stay put" when they come to the city. As sections of a city grew older, churches discovered that their members were moving to newer areas on the outskirts, leaving behind them a vacuum to be filled by newer arrivals. In the decades immediately after the Civil War most of the churches elected to follow their congregations by building new edifices in the areas to which their members had moved, and those churches which did not move often suffered a lingering death. Neither alternative, of course, provided an answer to the critical problem of providing a ministry in the areas which had been deserted by the older inhabitants. The answer that was beginning to receive strong support by 1880 was the institutional church.

Edward Judson defined an institutional church as "an organized body of Christian believers, who, finding themselves in a hard and uncongenial social environment, supplement the ordinary methods of the gospel—such as preaching, prayer meetings, Sunday school, and pastoral visitation—by *a system of organized kindness,* a congeries of institutions, which, by touching people on physical, social, and intellectual sides, will conciliate them and draw them within reach of the gospel."

Thus an institutional church was distinguished by its effort to adapt its program to the needs of its immediate neighborhood. Gymnasiums were built, evening classes organized, employment bureaus set up, loan associations established, medical clinics opened, public baths provided, nurseries for working mothers conducted, and clubs of all descriptions formed. The objective was to keep the church building open and in use at all hours every day and to draw the people of the neighborhood within its orbit.

The number of institutional churches rapidly multiplied during the last two decades of the nineteenth century, and their growth in membership was little short of phenomenal. Unfortunately, as the twentieth century advanced, the institutional churches became more and more absorbed in the social activities that originally were intended to provide a bridge into the life of the church, and as a result the ideal of mere humanitarian service replaced the earlier evangelistic concern. The consequence was a dwindling congregation with a mounting budget. In the end, far from being a means of building up a congregation to support a ministry in areas of deterioration, many institutional churches became social agencies for which other churches had to find money and leadership to maintain and support.

Religious education replaces revivalism.—Ever since the Great Awakening of the colonial era, revivalism had been the major method used to confront people with the claims of Christ and bring them into the life of the churches, but, after the Civil War, Dwight L. Moody was the last of the great revivalists. Moody himself became increasingly troubled by a growing awareness of a constantly declining response to his evangelistic campaigns. The changes that were taking place in the intellectual climate, the multiplying diversions and distractions of city life, and the increasing lack of homogeneity in the population were among the factors that combined to make revivals less and less successful. All other techniques devised by the churches to win the unchurched presupposed a primary reliance upon revivals to reach the great bulk of the people, and even those who were reached by other means were expected to take the final decisive step within the context of a revivalistic appeal. Thus when the revivals began to decline in effectiveness, the churches were faced with the necessity of finding some other basic standardized procedure for winning people to Christian truth and replenishing the ranks of their members.

The Sunday school seemed to offer the most promising alternative to revivalism as the conventional method for the recruiting of church members on the basis of a sound Christian experience. Since 1824 the missionaries of the American Sunday School Union had been busy establishing Sunday schools for the children of the nation, but after the Civil War the movement was carried forward in a new burst of enthusiasm and eager devotion by lay people. The Sunday School Union continued to exist, but the dynamic new agency was the International Sunday School Association, organized into city, county, state, and national conventions of Sunday school workers.

The movement was launched, at the suggestion of Dwight L. Moody, immediately after the close of the war. Although Moody furnished ideas, served on committees, enlisted support, and spoke in its behalf, the real architect of the movement was a Chicago real estate man and Baptist Sunday school superintendent, B. F. Jacobs. Described by his friends as "a steam engine of a man," Jacobs found time to pursue the indispensable organizational work with a relentless singleness of aim. He kept the various denominations working together harmoniously and also developed the efficient county convention system of bringing the Sunday school teachers together for periodic rallies, which constituted the real strength of the movement. His objective was to enlist, train, and inspire a vast host of Sunday school workers who would make a culminating "Decision Day" the focal point of their efforts. "To attend a convention revealed to the local worker his chosen cause operating on a larger field, broadened his fellowship, inspired him to new effort"; and, at the same time his ardor and zeal were being kindled, he was introduced to new methods and given a measure of training.

An innovation scarcely less significant than the convention system was the "Uniform Lesson" plan which was adopted, at the insistence of Jacobs, by the National Convention of 1872. Many advantages were claimed for the Uniform Lessons. Not the least was the fact that "next Sunday's lesson" provided a bond between the members of different denominations and contributed to the sense of Protestant solidarity. But the most important advantage of the Uniform plan was that it facilitated lesson-preparation for the teachers. It is reported that in such cities as New York, Boston, Buffalo, Cleveland, and Chicago, as many as eight to twelve hundred teachers would gather every Saturday afternoon to be instructed in the Uniform Lesson for the next day.

With the widespread support and popular enthusiasm that Jacobs had enlisted, the Sunday school was well-equipped to replace the older evangelism as a recruiting technique for those entering their teens. It still provided no means for reaching those in their later teens or adults. The "organized" class was a response to the need of the older teen-age and young adult group, and it was designed quite explicitly to serve as an instrument of evangelism. Each member of the class worked to win others for Christ and the church.

The organized class idea, with its slogan "each one win one," was originated by Marshall A. Hudson, of Syracuse, New York. He had noticed the young men who stood outside the doors of the church each Sunday, waiting for the girls who were teaching in the Sunday school; so he determined to win them by putting *them* to work for others. In 1890 he organized these young men into a Baraca (II Chron. 20:26) class, with their own officers, and an inner circle—"the secret service"—who were pledged to pray secretly each day for the members of the class who had not as yet made a Christian profession and "at a suitable time to speak to those for whom they [were] praying." The idea caught on, and soon classes were being organized in other churches. In 1895 Philathea (lovers of God) classes for young women were established. Within a short time national conventions were being held, and by 1913 the World-Wide Baraca-Philathea Union was composed of more than nine thousand classes with a membership of nearly one million in churches of thirty-two different denominations. But the Baracas and Philatheas were not the only nationally organized classes. Others quickly entered the field, among them being the Agoga and Amoma classes, the Drexel Biddle classes, the Bereans, the Gleaners, and the King's Daughters.

With the impetus provided by organized classes for youth, the Sunday school expanded into the adult field as well. By the turn of the century, most churches had adult Bible classes, which were frequently gathered around a striking personality whose name was given to the class. In 1905 the International Sunday School Association established an adult department to promote these classes and by 1908 it was issuing certificates of recognition to as many as six thousand new classes each year, and reminding them that "the chief business of this movement is the winning of souls to Jesus Christ."

The decline of revivalism, of course, could scarcely be regarded with equanimity by the churches, and it is not surprising that frenzied efforts were made by some to perpetuate it as a method for reaching the unchurched portions of the population —efforts which ultimately were to bring revivalism into almost complete disrepute. Protestants on the whole, however, had responded to the new situation with considerable imagination and resourcefulness. Of the specifically urban devices, the Y.M.C.A. alone was still reporting from two thousand to thirty-five hundred "hopeful conversions" each year at the turn of the century, but the institutional church and the specialized ministry to foreign-language groups had also displayed evidence of real strength. The primary reliance, however, was upon the Sunday school with its "Decision Days" for adolescents, organized classes for older young people, and Bible classes for adults. Vigorous and strong, enjoying popular support, and usually enlisting the ablest leadership of the community, the Sunday schools gave the churches what seemed to be real grounds for optimism as they looked to the future.

The churches discover the world.—Protestants did not limit the horizon of their concern to the United States. Not only the nation but the whole world was to be evangelized. American interest in foreign missions had first been aroused shortly after 1800 by news of English missionary activity and by firsthand reports from distant lands being brought back by the clipper ships. At the very moment when public attention was thus focused upon faraway places, the second Great Awakening was kindling new fervor and devotion among the people of the churches. Given these circumstances, it is not surprising that some of the more ardent and adventuresome of the youthful Christians should have felt an insistent summons to carry the gospel to the ancient lands of the East.

The earliest response was at Andover Theological Seminary, where a group of students banded together with the purpose of going as missionaries to the distant heathen. In 1810 they presented themselves to the Congregational General Association of Massachusetts with the result that the American Board of Commissioners for Foreign Missions was formed to undertake their support. The American churches, however, remained junior partners to the British until late in the nineteenth century. Then the roles were reversed, and the American churches surged forward.

During the later decades of the nineteenth century, Americans were becoming world-conscious, and in 1885 Josiah Strong, in a little book entitled *Our Country* sounded a clarion call for Americans to assume their responsibility for the Christianization of the world. The next year a student conference was held at Dwight L. Moody's base of operation in Northfield, Massachusetts. Before it was over an even one hundred had volunteered for foreign mission service, adopting the slogan: "The evangelization of the world in this generation." This was the birth of the Student Volunteer Movement, which for the next three decades was to enlist the ablest men and women on the college campuses of the nation and send them to the far corners of the earth.

The problem of providing support for these young people who were dedicating their lives in increasing numbers to foreign mission service was to become a serious one. A Presbyterian layman, John B. Sleman, Jr., sought to meet the need. He had attended a Student Volunteer Convention at Nashville in 1906 and was deeply moved by the thousands of students gathered there with one objective in mind. It seemed clear to him that the fields were ripe for the harvest and that the laborers were ready, but they did need to be sent. In the autumn of that year the Laymen's Missionary Movement was launched, and a nationwide campaign was undertaken to challenge laymen to match the devotion of youth with the dedication of their dollars. Until the outbreak of World War I, the Laymen's Missionary Movement was carried forward with the same surge of enthusiasm that characterized the Student Volunteer Movement.

Not only were churches established by these wide-ranging representatives of American Protestantism, but hospitals were built, schools and colleges founded, the culture and institutions of the West transmitted. Quite apart from their evangelistic efforts, the missionaries trained the leaders who were to spark the revolutionary ferment which swept these lands in the twentieth century. It was a daring venture that in some respects yielded a harvest of bitter fruit.

The halcyon years.—The decades bridging the turn of the century were the halcyon years of American Protestantism. In part this was due to the fact that Protestants shared the general cultural conviction of the time that they were living in the best of all possible worlds, but they did have some grounds for satisfaction. Churches were crowded; costly edifices were being built; programs were proliferating; the moral order, in public esteem if not always in practice, was unquestioned; a broad range of humanitarian concerns elicited widespread interest and generous support. Never before had the members of the churches exhibited so contagious an enthusiasm, and never before had they been so busy—serving in social settlements, organizing boys' clubs, teaching Sunday school classes, attending "open forums," and conducting campaigns. It was an era of crusades—"movements" they were called—which served to channel the unusual moral idealism and superabundance of zeal generated by the churches into a host of good causes.

These years were also the great age of the American pulpit. Sermons were often front-page news in the daily press, and those of some of the more prominent of the clergy were regularly syndicated nationally in their entirety. There was a whole galaxy of stars of national and even international reputation—Phillips Brooks, Russell Conwell, George A. Gordon, Washington Gladden, Lyman Abbott, Newell Dwight Hillis, Charles M. Sheldon, T. DeWitt Talmadge, Charles A. Parkhurst—and a host of others whose fame was regional. The preachers in general, James Bryce reported in his classic study of American society, were regarded as "first citizens," and they exercised "an influence often wider and more powerful than that of any layman."

By almost every outward standard of judgment, Protestants had good reason to be confident and assured, and for the most part they were. There were, of course, problems to be faced. A popular skepticism, stemming from new scientific hypotheses and typified by Robert G. Ingersoll, was manifesting itself in some quarters, but Protestants took comfort in the response which C. C. McCabe of the Methodist Church Extension Society had made to Ingersoll's taunt that "the churches are dying out all over the land." Upon reading Ingersoll's comment in the newspaper, McCabe dispatched a telegram which read:

American Protestantism

DEAR ROBERT:

All hail the power of Jesus' name—we are building more than one Methodist church for every day in the year, and propose to make it two a day!

C. C. McCABE

There was also an array of disturbing new social problems, but it was assumed that these, given time, would not be too difficult to resolve. Experience had taught Americans, Bryce reported, that "though the ascent of man may be slow it is also sure." Looking back over their past they could see "human nature growing gradually more refined, institutions better fitted to secure justice, the opportunities for happiness larger and more varied"; and looking ahead they saw "a long vista of years stretching out before them, in which they will have time enough to cure all their faults, to overcome all the obstacles that block their path."

It was still a Protestant America. Small islands of Roman Catholic population had been incorporated within the nation by successive annexations of territory, and a broadening tide of immigration had brought large Roman Catholic communities into being in the cities. The whole mood and spirit of the country, however, seemed so indelibly Protestant that in the end, it was confidently believed, all minority groups would be either assimilated or "Americanized." It was with some such conviction in mind that Leonard W. Bacon was able to report in 1897 that "the Catholic advance in America has not been, comparatively speaking, successful," and he cited the reassuring testimony of "an earnest Catholic from the once Catholic city of New Orleans that 'the nation, the government, the whole people, remain solidly Protestant.'"

These outward indications of Protestant strength and well-being, however, were deceptive. They represented little more than the high tide of a Protestant advance which had been carried forward by an accumulated momentum from the past, and the momentum was largely spent. In spite of the busyness of the churches the halcyon years of the two decades bridging the turn of the century actually marked the end of an era.

III

Protestantism in Post-Protestant

America, 1914——

Of all the symbols of nineteenth-century America, none was more characteristically Protestant than the Chautauqua Institution on Chautauqua Lake, which Theodore Roosevelt described as the most American thing in America. In similar vein he declared that he "would rather address a Methodist audience than any other audience in America," for "the Methodists represent the great middle class and in consequence are the most representative church in America." These random comments of a former President serve to highlight the dramatic shift in the religious complexion of the United States that occurred during the first fifty years of the twentieth century. In 1900 few would have disputed the contention that the United States was a Protestant nation, so self-evident was the fact that its life and its culture had been shaped by three centuries of Protestant witness and influence. But fifty years later so drastically had the situation changed that when Arnold S. Nash wrote the introductory chapter to a symposium *Protestant Thought in the Twentieth Century*, he gave it the title "America at the End of the Protestant Era."

To say that the United States had entered a post-Protestant era is not to deny that much of American culture continued to be informed by a distinctly Protestant ethos, nor is it to contend that Protestantism was no longer a factor shaping American life. It is simply to affirm that the United States had become a pluralistic society in which Protestantism had ceased to enjoy its old predominance and near monopoly in the religious life of the nation.

The post-Protestant era was in large part the product of the flood tide of immigration which poured into the United States during the last two decades of the nineteenth century and the first decade and a half of the twentieth century. Major Jewish communities came into existence in a number of cities, and the adherents of the several national churches of Eastern Orthodoxy formed significant clusters in some of the industrial centers. The most important shift in the population balance, however, was the result of the tremendous influx of Roman Catholic immigrants. At the time of the first census in 1790, Roman Catholics constituted less than 1 per cent of the population, some 30,000 out of 3,900,000. During the middle decades of the nineteenth century Roman Catholics began arriving in large numbers from Ireland and Germany, and toward the close of the century the Roman Catholic population was being vastly augmented by the great tide of immigration from central and southern Europe which reached its peak in the years immediately prior to 1914. By 1906 Roman Catholics constituted approximately 17 per cent of the population. Owing to problems of adjustment in a new land, including the isolation from the general cultural life imposed upon many of them by the language barrier, the influence of these new Americans was not to begin to be fully exerted until after World War I. Thereafter Roman Catholicism became an increasingly important factor in the life of the nation, and Protestantism was confronted by the difficult problem of adjusting itself to a status of coexistence with another major religious tradition.

The shift from a Protestant to a post-Protestant era in America, however, is not to be explained solely in numerical terms. The Protestant churches continued to claim almost twice as many members as the Roman Catholic church. Furthermore, the projection of a United States Census Bureau study in 1958 indicated that two-thirds of all Americans thought of themselves as Protestants, whereas only one-fourth thought of themselves as Roman Catholics. There are few informed observers, however, who would regard these figures as an accurate indication of the actual balance of influence exerted by these two religious traditions. Before the turn of the century the death of Phillips Brooks plunged the whole nation into mourning, but it was noted by a discerning interpreter in 1958 that it was no longer possible to imagine that "the death of any national Protestant leader or political figure other than the President himself would command the massive 'interfaith' attention which accompanied the death of Samuel Cardinal Stritch in 1958." Illustrations of this type could be multiplied, and they serve to document the fact that a more marked realignment of religious forces in the United States had taken place than the bare statistics suggest.

One of the factors contributing to the relative decline—in proportion to its numerical strength—of Protestant influence was the fact that Roman Catholic strength was centered in the cities, whereas the great stronghold of Protestantism had been centered in the small towns and villages of the countryside. Since the cities were the real power centers of twentieth-century America, these differing strongholds of the two traditions spell out in part the difference of impact they were able to exert. It was the concentration of strength in a few key cities which also explains to a considerable degree why the influence of the Jewish community was far out of proportion to its numbers. The relative weakness of Protestantism in the new situation is not to be understood solely by its dependence upon a dwindling farm and village civilization. It was due quite as much to internal factors which were the product of its peculiar historical development in the United States.

For a variety of reasons, Protestants did not find it easy to adjust to the necessities of a pluralistic society. They had possessed a near monopoly for so long that it came as a shock to discover that they were henceforth to live in a highly competitive situation in which many of the things they had taken for granted would be sharply challenged. This discovery alone was to be sufficiently demoralizing, but there were other factors that made it difficult for American Protestants to respond vigorously to the demands of a pluralistic society.

For one thing, Protestantism had become complacent. In a very real sense, it had become a victim of its own success. Throughout the nineteenth century the Protestant churches had been on the march, seeking to win men and women to the Christian faith, to penetrate the institutions of society with Christian principles, and to keep abreast of the retreating frontier. They had succeeded remarkably well and had brought into being a society and a culture that was recognizably Christian. By the end of the century, the final frontier areas had been "churched," and the American people seemed to be settling down to a stable churchgoing existence defined in Protestant terms. There were, as has been noted, non-Protestant enclaves in the cities, but given time it was assumed that these would be assimilated. Thus, at this critical juncture, the Protestant churches—pleased with the past and confident of the future—tended to relax. A mood of complacency was scarcely appropriate for the situation in which they were to find themselves as they moved forward into the new century, and it heightened the sense of shock they were to experience when they discovered just how inappropriate it was. But American Protestantism was suffering from a deeper malady.

The deeper malady was the theological erosion which had taken place during the nineteenth century. As has been suggested, a pluralistic society is a highly competitive society—a society in which various traditions are locked in debate. In such a situation, presuppositions must be clearly defined and their implications carefully articulated, if a particular religious grouping is to survive and make its influence felt. This means that the adherents of the several traditions must be knowledgeable and informed. They must be able to give both an account of and a reasoned defense for their faith, and they must be able to spell out its implications with clarity and persuasiveness. Otherwise they are not equipped to participate effectively in the discussion. It was precisely at this point that American Protestantism had become weak.

The theological erosion that had taken place was the product of several factors. It was in part the result of the absence of any sharp challenge to the Protestant understanding of the Christian faith, for in this situation fundamental assumptions tend to be taken for granted. Consequently the Protestant community had become increasingly composed of adherents whose religious affiliation was determined more by accident of birth and persistence of custom than by conscious conviction. It was also in part the product of the attrition to which every religious movement is subject. There is always an alternation between periods of spiritual quickening and vitality and periods of decline and lethargy. Any great surge of religious life and spiritual renewal is always followed by a gradual diminution of zeal and a fading of earlier imperatives. But there were other features of nineteenth-century Protestant life which accentuated and hastened the process.

Nineteenth-century Protestantism in America, as we have seen, was the heir of the great tide of Evangelical religion, stemming from the Great Awakening, which contributed the aggressive missionary spirit that gave to nineteenth-century Protestant Action its dynamic thrust. While the restless energy released by Evangelicalism succeeded in placing a Christian stamp on much of American culture, Evangelicalism by itself was not an unmixed blessing. Doctrinal definitions tended to be neglected in the stress that was placed upon "heart religion" and the "conversion experience." The demands of the Christian life, to be sure, continued to be spelled out within the framework of an earlier theological understanding, and so long as this theological structure persisted a formative influence was exerted upon society. But since the appeal of Evangelicalism was directed more to the emotions than to the intellect, the tendency was for the inherited capital to be lost.

The theological erosion was also accelerated by the particular technique—revivalism—which Evangelicalism developed as a means of winning men and women to Christian obedience. The revivalist faced at least two temptations. First, he was tempted to reduce the ambiguities of human life and the complexities of the Christian faith to simple alternatives so that he could issue a clear-cut call for decision. Second, he was tempted to stress results and to justify whatever tended to produce them. As a result of these two pressures, the tendency of the revivalist was to over simplify the issues, and the ultimate consequence as the century moved toward its close was to contribute to those forces which were emptying the faith of American Protestantism of its content. It should be acknowledged that the temptations implicit in revivalism were resisted with varying degrees of success by the greater revivalists, for they were men acutely sensitive to the hazards and uncertainties of the road to salvation. But often this sensitivity was lacking.

The energetic busyness of the churches during the latter part of the century had done little to arrest the erosion. Members were added to the churches. Moral idealism was generated, enthusiasm elicited, and people were put to work. But the basic theological task continued to be neglected. While a cluster of relatively vague and ill-defined folk beliefs survived in most of the churches and were perpetuated by the Uniform Lessons of the Sunday schools, few Protestants were aware of possessing a comprehensive, coherent, and clearly defined intellectual structure which would help to preserve their identity within the general culture and provide them with an independent perspective of their own. Stripped of this type of self-definition, Protestantism was in no position to meet either the challenge of the world or the challenge of other religious traditions with a sharp challenge of its own. Indeed, its tendency was to lose itself within the larger society which it had helped fashion.

· 9 ·

PROTESTANTISM'S LOSS OF IDENTITY

Apart from its busyness, the most conspicuous feature of American Protestantism as it moved toward the close of the nineteenth century had been its loss of identity. The theological erosion of earlier decades had dismantled its historic intellectual defenses, and the way was open to a rather complete assimilation of Protestantism to the model of the world. As a result, by the end of the century, American Protestantism had become more the creature of American culture than its creator. As Francis P. Miller was later to observe, a process which began with a culture being "molded by religious faith" was to end with a religious faith being "molded by a national culture."

The transition to a culture religion.—The assimilation was a complex and many-faceted process. It had begun under the aegis of the "romanticism" of popular Evangelicalism. While Evangelicalism in general, with its stress upon feeling rather than doctrine, tended to undermine the theological foundation of a self-consciously formulated social and cultural ethic, the "romanticism" of popular Evangelicalism denied the necessity for such an ethic. It operated on the assumption that converted individuals would automatically produce a Christian society and a Christian culture. As early as 1842, however, Francis Wayland had pointed out that if Christians are not provided with specific instruction on the implications of the Christian faith for the whole of life, they will nonetheless be instructed. In the absence of guidance from the churches, he insisted, they will derive their instruction from the prevailing standards of the market place, the political forum, and society at large.

Assimilation on this practical level was steady but not unduly rapid, for the unspent momentum of old ideas and impulses continued to exert their influence through habit, custom, and lingering sentiment. These habits and customs and sentiments, however, provided little guidance for the new type of corporate business activity that began to dominate American economic life after the Civil War. The assimilation, which the abdication of popular Evangelicalism made possible, can therefore be seen most clearly and dramatically in the dispatch with which even traditionalist evangelical Protestants embraced the free-wheeling ideas and ideals that were being fostered by a burgeoning industrial society. And then, by a curious twist, they took a further step which enabled them to re-establish the connection between faith and practice. Because these current ideas and ideals seemed to be blessed by the tangible benefits of an astonishing material prosperity, they concluded that the laissez faire code of the developing industrial society actually represented God's way of doing things. Thus, almost by inadvertence, the churches were led to sanctify the existing economic order and to lend themselves to an uncritical defense of the social status quo.

Even without the surrender to "romanticism," the folk beliefs which survived the process of theological erosion were too attenuated to have provided an independent ethic. Indeed, they were powerless to prevent a much more radical assimilation at the theological level. The reverse twist by which the connection between faith and practice was re-established in the economic order, with the mind of God being defined to conform to the practices of the business community, illustrates the general pattern of cultural assimilation. With their traditional theological insights emasculated, American Protestants were easily tempted to regard current cultural convictions as "self-evident" facts which disclosed the divine intention. While the resulting adjustment of the faith to the culture took many different forms, it found its most typical expression in what was loosely described as "the New Theology."

The New Theology.—The New Theology was essentially a culture religion with a single fundamental theological idea— the doctrine of the Incarnation, interpreted as divine immanence which sanctified the "natural" man and invested the culture itself with intrinsic redemptive tendencies. The burst of technological and industrial expansion which followed the Civil War had created an unbridled cheerfulness, confidence, and complacency among the American people. It was the Horatio Alger era of seemingly unlimited opportunity, and middle-class America at least was quite sure that it was living in the best of all possible worlds. This temper was reflected and further fortified among Protestants by a growing conviction that the mission of Christianity had been fulfilled in churchgoing America. It was this mood of complacent and self-confident optimism that was expressed in the New Theology.

Henry Ward Beecher, one of the earliest and most conspicuous exponents of the New Theology, informed the theological students at Yale in 1872 that the great task of the clergy was not to "go back and become apostles of the dead past," but rather to "make their theological systems conform to the facts as they are." This had been his own procedure, and it had led him to a blunt and emphatic rejection of any notion of a stern and demanding God. Out of his own experience and observation, he had discovered a benevolent deity who laid upon men no burdens heavier than they could bear. This God, whose nature it was to love men, not "out of compliment to Christ" but "from the fullness of a great heart," had made man "to start and not to stop, to go on and on, and up and onward, steadily emerging from the controlling power of the physical and animal condition in which he was born and which enthrall him during his struggle upward, but ever touching higher elements of possibility, and ending in the glorious liberty of sons of God." Beecher was equally convinced that Christianity should be defined in terms of "disposition and conduct," since "greatheartedness is more akin to the Gospel spirit than dogma or doctrine." It was not necessary, he insisted, to ask people what they believed as a condition of church membership, for doctrine is of little consequence if the results are good. And Beecher was confident that the results would quite inevitably be good, being guaranteed by the influence of American culture which had implanted "an ineradicable belief" among Americans that "Christian morality is the safe road from childhood to manhood."

Few were as blunt as Beecher in his break with the past. The more conventional response was quietly to bid the older doctrines good-bye without bothering to refute them. This was true of Phillips Brooks, who, with never failing charm and power, summoned people to share his simple faith in the spirit of man as the candle of the Lord, revealing God in human life. "Only a person can truly utter a person," he declared. "Whoever has in him the human quality, whoever has the spirit of man, has the candle of the Lord." This enthusiasm for humanity was his basic theme. "The ultimate fact of human life is goodness and not sin." This is true because

there is nothing in religion, there is nothing in Christianity, which has not its roots in human nature and in the fundamental affections of mankind. Utterly swept out of our thought must be any old contradiction between the graces of the gospel and the natural affections. . . . Believe in yourselves and reverence your own human nature; it is the only salvation from brutal vice and every false belief. . . . An optimist is a believer in the best, and any man who believes that anything less than the best is the ultimate purpose of God, and so the ultimate possibility of God's children, has no business to live upon the earth.

Like Beecher, Phillips Brooks found structural support for his faith in his supreme confidence in the power of the culture itself to nurture the natural Christian graces which were resident in every human heart. "I do not know how a man can be an American, even if he is not a Christian, and not catch something with regard to God's purpose as to this great land."

The most impressive feature of American life, to Brooks, was "the effort of men to do outside the churches and outside Christianity that which the churches and Christianity undertake to do." Thus even "the spirit of the world feels the desire of the things the church means, and tries to do them . . . in another way."

What mean all the secular, all the studiously irreligious, all the even blasphemous attempts at education and the development of character? What mean the efforts of philanthropy that studiously disown anything except political economy as the impulse from which they work? . . . What do they mean except that that which Christianity intends the human heart desires . . . ?

This confidence in "the great human impulse, which is the divine impulse," expressing itself in and in turn being nurtured by "the spirit of the world," was the secret of Brooks's broad-churchmanship. Humanity itself, not any organized body of believers, is God's instrument, and through humanity itself God effects his purposes. This is the true church, embracing the whole of mankind, the entire family of God. It is a church without organization, discipline, or ritual, but it is a church in which "the great human impulses" lead men to do "Christian work in the spirit of Christ" even when they "studiously" or "vehemently" disown him.

The most striking feature of the New Theology was its lack of normative content, its surrender of any independent basis of judgment. By means of its doctrine of Incarnation, Christ was identified with what were conceived to be the finest cultural ideals and the noblest cultural institutions. Thus it was compatible with every conceivable social attitude, with whatever stream of secular thought one might wish to support and consecrate, with whatever system of values might seem good in the light of one's own personal predilections. In many ways, because the culture was reasonably Christian, the New Theology was reasonably Christian, but it offered little independent wisdom and guidance to the Christian believer. Men of differing temperaments and differing backgrounds held differing opinions about what constituted the best of the cultural "goods" and thus were led to select as of primary importance in the economy of Christ differing aspects of the existing culture. Thus Brooks —a natural aristocrat—was opposed to any leveling of the classes which would prevent men from living together harmoniously in an interesting and enriching inequality. Beecher—an exuberant clerical entrepreneur—was convinced that poverty was the product of wilful sin. Russell H. Conwell—schooled in the marts of trade and instructed by the folklore of Horatio Alger—believed that everyone had an opportunity and a Christian duty to become a millionaire. A sensitive-spirited Washington Gladden, on the other hand, having personally encountered the distress occasioned by a strike of millhands at North Adams, Massachusetts, believed that current experience amply testified to the fact that "the law of nature" is "the law of brotherhood." He was convinced that this law was manifesting itself in the pressures of American economic life and subjecting men to a compulsion to co-operate and to live together in a true brotherly relationship of mutual help and service.

The second striking feature of the New Theology was the way in which its proponents invested the cultural or social process itself with intrinsic redemptive tendencies, thus reflecting the general mood of satisfaction with things as they were or were about to become. The basic confidence might be Brooks's "great human impulses" which lead men to do God's work even when they disown him; it might be Conwell's "inspired, sanctified, common sense of enterprising business men" that was operating to make the world more Christlike; or it might be Gladden's conviction that the inexorable march of events was ushering in a day of enlightened self-interest and brotherhood. But, however it was identified, the fundamental assumption was the same—that somehow the guarantee was "natural" and inherent in the process itself. Thus little room was left for any special redemptive work of Christ.

A third feature of the New Theology was the fading of any real distinction between the church and the world. Those who accepted its basic assumptions found it difficult to conceive of a church that did not embrace humanity indiscriminately. They had emphasized disposition and conduct as the essence of religion in order to ease their departure from the inherited faith and to facilitate the adjustment to a new set of theological convictions. But the new convictions did not provide any criteria for ethical discrimination, and consequently even at the point of conduct the possibility of a distinction between the church and the world was ruled out.

The effect of the New Theology was to cut the nerve of the evangelistic impulse. If men are naturally religious and the culture or society tends to foster the natural Christian graces, the absence of those graces indicates a defect, not in the individual, but in the culture or the society. Washington Gladden rejoiced that the "conversion of sinners" was no longer "supposed to be the preacher's main business," and Edward Judson, son of the famous missionary to Burma, declared: "The important thing is not the building up of a church but the Christianization of society."

There was a difference of opinion, to be sure, on the extent to which society needed to be reformed. Phillips Brooks and Russell H. Conwell were content to take their stand with things pretty much as they were. Washington Gladden, on the other hand, was convinced that a major reconstruction of society was being forced upon the nation. Between these two extremes were people interested in particular reforms as universal panaceas for the ills of society—the elimination of poverty, disease, illiteracy, crime, vice, political corruption, and irreligion by the suppression of the liquor traffic, or by giving the vote to women. Others believed that to meet immediate human needs— recreational, educational, medical, and economic—by enlightened philanthropy was all that was needed.

A vivid illustration of this new conception of the task of the churches is found in the response that was made to facts disclosed in 1897 by a survey of the fifteenth assembly district in Manhattan. The survey, sponsored by the Federation of Churches and Christian Workers of New York City, revealed that one-half of the forty thousand persons in the district neither belonged to nor attended any church. Even more startling was the fact that the ten Protestant churches in the area had a total membership of only 1,798. Two years later a report listed the results which had been achieved by "the organized intelligence and love of our churches" having been brought to bear upon the situation. Kindergartens, clubs, and cooking schools had been started, public baths opened, libraries and a new park established, and "one of the most active and successful industrial settlements in the city" had been organized.

What was most astonishing about the emergence of the New Theology is that its appearance aroused so little dissent. So long as it involved nothing more than the echoing of the current cultural convictions which expressed the general sense of well-being, not even the most conservative Protestants seem to have been alarmed by its implicit repudiation of historic Protestantism. Opposition appeared only when a further step was taken in an effort to come to terms with the new intellectual currents which were bringing into question the accepted understanding of biblical authority.

The Modernist-Fundamentalist controversy.—By the second decade of the twentieth century, Protestants had become embroiled in a bitter theological controversy. The protagonists were the "Liberals" or "Modernists," who sought to adjust the inherited faith to the new intellectual climate, and the "Fundamentalists," who insisted that the old ways of stating the faith must be preserved unimpaired. It may seem somewhat arbitrary to distinguish the developing biblical "liberalism" from the older New Theology, for many of the more conspicuous exponents of the New Theology were ultimately to embrace the conclusions being reached by the "scientific" investigators. This was notably true of Beecher and Gladden. But there were others who showed little interest in academic questions. Conwell, for example, was quite content to continue preaching his

Gospel of Wealth without giving more than passing notice to biblical texts.

The two movements, perhaps, can best be distinguished by suggesting that the New Theology reflected the general popular climate of opinion, while "liberalism" sought to grapple with the issues being raised in more specifically intellectual currents of thought. The former was primarily a preacher's theology, being fashioned in the pulpit, whereas the latter was basically the product of the academic concerns of professors in colleges and theological seminaries and only gradually became incorporated in the fare of the pulpit. Washington Gladden illustrated the earlier process when he reported that his "theology had to be hammered out on the anvil of daily use in the pulpit. The pragmatic test was the only one that could be applied to it: 'Will it work?' " Henry Ward Beecher confessed that he had developed his theology in much the same way. He wanted to get results, and he discovered that they could be secured by finding a truth with which all his hearers agreed and then pressing it home with an intense personal application and appeal. "I gradually formed a theology by practice," he declared, "—by trying it on, and the things that really did God's work in the hearts of men I set down as good theology, and the things that did not, whether they were true or not, they were not true to me." The latter phase developed when the "danger" was recognized, as Beecher put it, "of having the intelligent part of society go past us." "The providence of God," he continued, "is rolling foward in a spirit of investigation that Christian ministers must meet and join. There is no class of people upon earth who can less afford to let the development of truth run ahead of them."

The new intellectual currents are familiar enough, having

been repeatedly described in detail. New scientific discoveries and hypotheses, most notably the concept of evolution, posed new problems of biblical interpretation and tended to undermine accepted notions of biblical authority. New methods of textual and historical criticism raised similar questions and created further uncertainties. The psychology of religion came into its own as a respectable academic discipline which could be utilized to explain religious experience as mere "wish-fulfillment." Sociological studies were not initially so disturbing, but they were distracting, for they emphasized how to get things done by manipulating the external environment. These sociological studies, dealing with the everyday aspects of life at first-hand, were intensely absorbing, and in the end they were to be of crucial significance in interpreting the faith as a social phenomenon and the church as a mere social agency.

American Protestants were ill-prepared to cope with this headlong rush into a new intellectual world. Their whole religious outlook having been shaped by the non-intellectual concerns of Evangelicalism, they were not equipped to do much more than either appropriate uncritically the conclusions of supposedly objective scholarship or, as the other alternative, reject them out-of-hand. Those of urban middle-class America whose traditional faith had been eroded by the New Theology found it easy to make the adjustment to the new intellectual climate, but those whose memories were stirred by the language and practices of religious life in small-town and rural America tended to adopt an obscurantist stance. The theologians in the seminaries were the first to deal with the problem systematically. By the very nature of their assignment, they labored under the necessity to restate the Christian faith in terms intellectually defensible and convincing. They strove manfully, as the repeated editions of their systematic theologies amply testify, to find a middle way that would do justice both to the claims of the faith and modern thought, but the whole apparatus of what remained of the inherited doctrinal structure seemed suddenly archaic and out-of-date.

It is somewhat difficult to characterize adequately the "Liberals" or "Modernists" who sought to reconcile the Christian faith with "modern" ways of thinking, for they represented no solid phalanx and at least a half-dozen different solutions to the problem can be identified. The key issue was the authority of the Bible, for Protestantism historically claimed the authority of Scripture for the whole structure of its thought. Furthermore, it was a highly explosive issue when directly raised, since Protestant piety expressed itself most characteristically in daily Bible-reading as the focal point of family devotions and thus it was in the Bible enshrined on the "family altar" that the deepest emotions of Protestants were centered. The modernist tendency, as exhibited in such men as Shailer Mathews and G. B. Foster, was to reverence the Bible as a treasury of religious devotion but to reject it as being in any sense normative in religion. It was a suitable subject for historical study and useful for devotional purposes, but the canons of truth were to be found elsewhere. Thus the Modernists represented a tendency to forget that the Christian faith had any claim of its own to truth, and many of them came to depend, for their basic affirmations, upon what was often described as the unfolding revelation of God to be found in the scientific study of man, society, and the natural world. For them, the real theologians—the men who served as arbiters of Christian truth and made plain the mind of God—were no longer in the theological seminaries. They were the autonomous scholars in the universities who stood outside the faith in terms of their intellectual inquiries.

It is equally difficult to characterize adequately the "fundamentalist" reaction to the modernist tendencies, for Fundamentalism also represented diverse tendencies. Those associated with Curtis Lee Laws, editor of the *Watchman-Examiner*, who first coined the term and applied it to themselves in 1920, probably can best be described as genuine "conservatives," whose intention was to conserve and defend the integrity and continuity of the Christian faith. They centered their attention on the question of biblical authority and did not wish to make an issue of either evolution or biblical inerrancy. They represented the type of reaction to the more extreme modernist tendencies that had long been present in Protestant seminaries and which was perhaps best represented by Augustus Hopkins Strong, who had affirmed that "neither evolution nor the higher criticism has any terrors to one who regards them as parts of Christ's creating and education process," but who also insisted that to abandon the Bible as the authoritative testimony to Christ and thus in a derivative sense the authoritative ground of faith would be to cut the "taproot" and imperil the very existence of Protestantism.

Even before the term was coined, this moderate or conservative Fundamentalism had been largely displaced by a belligerent anti-Modernist reaction stemming from the "Prophetic" Bible conferences of the latter part of the nineteenth century. The premillennial views enunciated at these conferences presupposed the verbal inspiration of Scripture in every detail as the basis for their whole system, and consequently the itinerant revivalists who found their inspiration at the conferences were quick to assail all forms of biblical liberalism. Christian orthodoxy was identified with biblical inerrancy, and was tested by whether or not one accepted literally the Genesis account of creation, the virgin birth of Jesus, his substitutionary atonement, physical resurrection, and imminent bodily return to earth. The "social gospel" views of Washington Gladden which many of the biblical liberals had adopted constituted a double affront to this group because the "social gospel" represented an explicit and forthright rejection of their premillennial convictions.

Whatever the intentions of its more moderate wing, Fundamentalism can probably best be understood as a phase of the rural-urban conflict, representing the tendency of many who were swept into a strange new urban environment to cling to the securities of their childhood in rural America. In this sense, Fundamentalism was much more cultural than religious in its orientation, and frequently exhibited, as H. Richard Niebuhr has observed, "a greater concern for conserving the cosmological and biological notions of older cultures than for the Lordship of Jesus Christ." Equally significant is the fact that Fundamentalism consistently aligned itself with "ultra-conservative political, economic, and social views," while the mores which were associated with Christ had "at least as little relation to the New Testament and as much connection with social custom" as did those of its opponents. Actually the five or six "fundamentals" for which the Fundamentalists were ready to do battle were scarcely adequate to spell out a full-orbed understanding of the Christian life and, in the absence of a fully developed theological structure, such a conspicuous representative of Fundamentalism as Billy Sunday tended to equate "salvation with decency, patriotism, and manliness."

The publication of twelve small volumes of *The Fundamen-*

tals between 1909 and 1912 marked the transformation of Fundamentalism from a movement of dissent into a power group intent on seizing control of the various Protestant denominations. It is perhaps significant that the publication of these volumes was financed by two wealthy laymen at a time when the "social gospel" movement was at its height. The struggle for control of Protestant educational institutions, missionary enterprises, and denominational machinery reached its climax in the 1920's. Strategies and techniques varied from denomination to denomination, but the obscurantism, violent language, and "smear" tactics of the more vociferous of the Fundamentalists so alienated public opinion generally that Fundamentalism failed to capture a single major Protestant denomination. But neither did the Modernists win. Alarmed by the threat to institutional concerns that was being created by the divisive struggle, denominational politicians took charge and, supported by the great mass of church people, succeeded in silencing the controversy. Theological discussion tended to be ruled out of bounds in the interest of united support for denominational programs, and there was a renewed emphasis upon "disposition and conduct" as the only satisfactory test of religious faith.

The acceptance of a community church status.—By 1930, with theological issues having been brushed under the carpet, the churches of the major old-line Protestant denominations had settled down to a relatively peaceful and non-controversial existence as "community" churches. This transition in status from "gathered" churches to "community" churches has been implicit in the basic assumptions of the New Theology. With the obliteration of any real distinction between the church and the world, as has been noted, it became difficult to conceive of a church which did not embrace humanity indiscriminately.

This fading distinction had the further consequence of making it difficult to view denominational differences as much more than anachronistic sectarian survivals. From a practical point of view, with almost all theological criteria having been ruled out, there was little possibility of defending denominational differences as belonging within the realm of a necessary Christian obedience, while from a theoretical point of view the basic presupposition of "the 'evangelical' doctrine that schism is the normal condition of the church of Christ" in this fallen world had been rejected. Thus there was little reason why the whole community should not be embraced within one church, and there was at least one compelling reason why it should be. If the church was unable to distinguish itself in any fundamental fashion from the world at large, it could at least bear witness to the essential oneness of humanity. It should therefore be a center of fellowship which would give visible expression to the unity of the community.

The community church idea had found its earliest expression in the organization of non-denominational churches by residents of new suburban areas who desired only one church for their community. These non-denominational community churches were immensely popular, but they labored under several handicaps. The two most obvious handicaps were their inability to draw upon denominational resources to help finance the construction of church buildings and their inability to command a readily available source of ministers. Many ministers, for example, were unwilling to give up the security provided by both denominational pension plans and many were fearful lest the absence of established procedures for being transferred from one post to another should leave them stranded when a change might seem desirable. As a result of these handicaps, the non-denominational churches were in no position to compete effectively when the denominations, not content to acquiesce in their own demise, adopted the community church idea as an integral part of their church extension programs.

To implement their community church program, the major old-line Protestant denominations devised "comity" agreements whereby a new suburban area would be assigned to a single denomination with the understanding that it would seek to minister to all the religious needs of that community. Other areas, of course, were assigned on a similar basis to other denominations. At the same time that Community Methodist and Community Baptist churches were being organized in the suburbs, the churches in the older established areas were seeking to embody the community church ideal by announcing that they were "friendly" churches and equally "ecumenical" in their readiness to welcome adherents of other denominations into their membership. The curious phenomenon developed of a member of a Presbyterian church, for example, exclaiming: "I am not really a Presbyterian; I have always been a Methodist."

The Congregationalists were the most forthright in defining their churches as community churches. A history of Congregationalism, published by that denomination's press, was to declare that "a Congregational church is a group of Christians associated together for a definite purpose, not because of peculiarities of belief," and that members of these churches "are not asked to renounce their previous denominational teachings but are asked to join in a simple covenant pledging cooperation and fellowship." This point of view was further elaborated in a pamphlet issued by the Commission on Evangelism and Devotional Life of the Congregational Christian Churches, which asserted that Congregationalists "have seen the need for churches which shall meet the religious requirements of *all* the people in a given community. . . . A Congregational community church is a place of friendly cooperative Christian enterprise that fits the mood and standards of a community. Its membership is open to all."

The vagueness which surrounded the concept of "friendly cooperative Christian enterprise" can best be seen in the shift of emphasis in the missionary outreach of the churches. City missions, for example, had been established as evangelistic centers for reaching the unchurched portions of the population, but by the 1920's they had been largely transformed into social agencies. This transition had been fostered by a study sponsored by the influential Institute of Social and Religious Research, which had concluded its report with the recommendation: "A decreasing emphasis upon specific church program and intensification of efforts to help the immigrant worker in the struggle for economic security and social recognition suggest themselves as the most constructive items on the future program of mission work." The same trend was apparent in foreign missions where an increasing stress was being placed upon the dissemination of technological, agricultural, medical, and educational knowledge and skills as the primary task of the missionary, while some influential supporters of the mission enterprise were quite explicit in suggesting that the idea of Christian evangelization should be replaced with the concept of intercultural penetration.

Much of the shift to a community-oriented faith, to be sure, was quite unconscious, and few churches announced that the Christian gospel had been trimmed to fit "the mood and standards" of the community, but it is clear that Protestantism, as represented by the major old-line denominations, was losing its identity and no longer possessed to any great degree the indispensable leverage of an independent theological position which formerly had enabled it to exert a creative and effective influence in society. The average church member was convinced that the church was something to be supported along with other good causes, but neither the intellectual or ethical implications of the faith he professed extended much beyond the patterns of thought and behavior already current in society.

With church life being sustained more by habit and custom than by a conscious commitment to "Christian" truth, the most characteristic response to the competitive situation presented by a pluralistic society was the growing conviction among many Protestants that one religion is as good as another, that it is impertinent to raise divisive issues, that it does not make much difference what one believes so long as he is sincere, and that men of differing faiths by their different routes are all headed for the same place and striving for the same ends. This mood—"religion in general" it has been called—penetrated Roman Catholicism and Judaism as well as Protestantism during these years, and to the extent that it penetrated these communities their influence was emasculated. But, because of the theological erosion to which it had been subjected and because of the absence of social factors tending to create a group consciousness and solidarity, Protestantism suffered most from this pervasive climate of opinion.

· 10 ·

THE NEW CONFIGURATION OF AMERICAN PROTESTANTISM

The major old-line Protestant denominations remained the overwhelmingly dominant current in American Protestantism until well into the twentieth century. They had early been shaped to a common pattern and had emerged from the controversies of the fourth and fifth decades of the nineteenth century somewhat altered in outlook but still retaining their essential homogeneity. While a reshuffling in numerical rank had occurred, they continued to exhibit a remarkable uniformity in their understanding of the Christian faith. During the decades bridging the turn of the twentieth century, they had been subjected about equally to the impact of the New Theology and the strains of the Modernist-Fundamentalist controversy. While there was some variation in response to this dual pressure, the basic adjustment which they effected was much the same.

Diverse tendencies had become apparent in two or three of these denominations, but a stranger moving from one church to another in the middle decades of the twentieth century would still have had difficulty identifying the denominational affiliation of most of them by the sermons that were preached, the hymns that were sung, the architecture of the buildings, the order of worship, and the schedule of weekday activities. Even the organizational pattern of local churches was almost indistinguishable. This basic similarity was reflected in the ease with which people moved from one of these denominations to another, with their membership and to a degree their ministry becoming quite freely interchangeable.

In spite of the continuing homogeneity of most of the old-line denominations, American Protestantism as a whole was losing much of its unity and cohesiveness during the first half of the twentieth century. Some groups, such as the Lutherans, which hitherto had played only a minor role in Protestant life were becoming much more prominent, and a few denominations were changing in character. This shift in character was most conspicuous among Southern Baptists and Episcopalians. Southern Baptists had been infiltrated by a group which insisted that Baptists were not Protestants and that Protestant churches were not Christian churches. While this sentiment was not predominant among Southern Baptists, it was sufficiently strong to inhibit Southern Baptist participation in co-operative activities. In similar fashion, a strong party had developed within the Protestant Episcopal Church which insisted that Episcopalians were not Protestants and belonged instead wholly within the "Catholic" tradition. Quite apart from this insistence which occasionally made it difficult for Episcopalians to participate in Protestant activities, the Episcopalians had been moving increasingly in the direction of a more "sacramental" conception of church life that was at marked variance with the remaining "evangelical" characteristics of much of Protestantism. But the most notable shift in twentieth-century Protestantism was represented by the emergence of three new sizable groups which differed greatly in temper and spirit from the older major denominations. Thus American Protestantism had become much more multiform and diverse than it had ever been before in its history. This, in turn, greatly complicated the problem of self-definition and contributed to Protestantism's loss of identity.

The shifting denominational pattern of American Protestantism.—According to statistics compiled for the *Yearbook of the American Churches for 1960*, there were approximately 59,-332,000 members of Protestant churches in the United States in 1958. A careful analysis of these statistics gives a rather clear picture of the altered shape of American Protestantism in terms of the following major groups:

American Protestantism

1. Baptists 18,547,844
2. Methodists 12,758,346
3. Lutherans 7,791,248
4. Fundamentalists 4,428,033
5. Presbyterians 4,117,261
6. Episcopalians 3,042,286
7. Holiness groups 2,521,648
8. Disciples of Christ 1,943,599
9. Congregationalists 1,381,124
10. Evangelical and Reformed ... 806,365
11. Adventists 332,965

Among the larger groups representing the remaining 1,660,000 Protestants were: Salvation Army, 250,583; Reformed Church of America, 216,096; Church of the Brethren, 200,282; Mennonites, 156,230; and Friends, 120,766.

Among the significant shifts reflected in these figures is the drop in numerical ranking since 1850 of the Congregationalists from fourth to ninth place, of the Presbyterians from third to fifth, of the Disciples of Christ from sixth to eighth, and of the Methodists from first to second. The Baptists had advanced from second to first place primarily as a result of a surge of growth by Southern Baptists. The Episcopalians moved from seventh to sixth place, but in the interim they had shifted the basis of reporting their membership from the number of communicants to the number of baptized. The Lutherans had exchanged places with the Presbyterians, moving from fifth to third place. Actually Lutheran growth was much greater than this shift in numerical rank would suggest, for they had multiplied their number forty-eight times while the Presbyterians were achieving only a ninefold increase. Much more significant than their increase in numbers, however, was the larger influence which Lutherans had begun to exert in American Protestantism as a whole.

Although Lutherans had grown rapidly in numbers throughout the nineteenth century as a result of mounting influx of German and Scandinavian immigrants, they had remained isolated from American life and, with the exception of Princeton-educated Samuel S. Schmucker, whose efforts were repudiated by most of his fellow Lutherans, not a single Lutheran exerted any effective leadership in Protestantism as a whole until after World War I. There were several reasons why the Lutherans should have contributed so little during these years to the general character of American Protestantism. The most obvious was the language barrier which Lutherans often sought to perpetuate as a means of preserving their European cultural heritage by making the process of assimilation and integration into American life more difficult. Furthermore, they were so engrossed in establishing congregations among newly arrived immigrants that they had little time or energy for broader concerns and quite inevitably tended to become self-centered, insular, and provincial in outlook. Lastly, they were badly fragmented into many different groups representing differing national backgrounds, differing tides of immigration, differing areas of settlement, and some differences of theological conviction.

After World War I, when large-scale immigration had come to an end and the existing churches were no longer so overwhelmed by the mere task of attempting to provide a ministry for the vast influx of new arrivals, Lutherans began to play a more active role in American life. The language barrier was difficult to maintain beyond the first generation in urban centers, and the emotions aroused by the war had hastened the abandonment of the former efforts to perpetuate it. Intermarriage with non-Lutherans became more frequent and many of the churches began to become aware of their responsibility to unchurched neighbors of other than Lutheran background. The period following World War I also witnessed a general rapprochement among the scattered Lutheran groups. In 1917 three Norwegian groups were brought together to form the Evangelical Lutheran Church; in 1918 three German bodies united to form the United Lutheran Church; and in 1930 three other German synods came together to form the American Lutheran Church. In 1960 seven Lutheran groups voted to participate in two further mergers, with the result that almost all Lutherans belonged to one of three major bodies—the Lutheran Church in America with approximately three million members; the Lutheran Church–Missouri Synod with more than two and a quarter million members; and the American Lutheran Church with slightly less than two and a quarter million members. By this time, as a result of these several factors, Lutheranism had become a strong force in American life, had given an added dimension to Protestantism in the public mind, and was contributing influential theological and ecclesiastical leadership to American Protestantism as a whole.

What was true of Lutherans was also true of other Protestant groups with a Continental background. The Church of the Brethren, for example, had emerged from its former isolation and had become a fully participating member of the National Council of Churches. The Evangelical and Reformed Church—the product of the merger of the German Reformed Church with the Evangelical Synod in 1934—was by far, with the exception of the Lutheran churches, the largest and most influential of the Continental bodies. The German Reformed had made the adjustment to American life much more rapidly than the Lutherans and by the middle of the nineteenth century they were beginning to produce what was to become a notable succession of distinguished theologians. Thus they were making a significant contribution at the same time that they were becoming more fully identified with American Protestant life. This latter process culminated in 1957, when the General Synod of the Evangelical and Reformed Church and the General Council of the Congregational Christian Churches voted to unite to form the United Church of Christ. Although the Evangelical United Brethren Church did not represent a non-indigenous Protestant tradition, the merger of the two German Methodist groups in 1946, which brought into being a church of three-quarters of a million members, made it possible for this formerly German-speaking denomination to assume a much more influential role within the general context of American Protestant life.

The most conspicuous new element in the changed configuration of American Protestantism, however, was the emergence in the twentieth century of the strong Fundamentalist, Holiness, and Adventist groupings, which in their general conservatism had much in common and which together totaled more than seven million adherents. One of the most difficult problems is to classify adequately the miscellaneous bodies which fall within this threefold category, for they often can be distinguished only by emphasis. The great majority of these groups looked for a triumphant return of Christ, but because their major stress was upon this doctrine, the Adventist group is restricted to the two bodies (Seventh-day Adventists and Advent Christian Church) which stemmed from the Millerite excitement of 1843–44. The Fundamentalist groups placed a primary emphasis upon the "fundamentals" as defined during the first two decades of the twentieth century, but they were divided by differing denominational, theological, and cultural traditions. The Holiness groups were basically "fundamentalist" in doctrine, but in addition they emphasized most strongly the Wesleyan concept of a second baptism of the Spirit which results in an "entire sanctification." The Holiness group, in turn, was divided into two wings—the purely "perfectionist" bodies and the Pentecostal groups which insisted that the baptism of the Spirit is also accompanied by the gifts of the Spirit, most notably "speaking in tongues."

The Holiness groups began to emerge during the 1880's, but they did not gain real strength until the twentieth century. They represented the continuing heritage of the Holiness movement which was basically Methodist in background but which swept through many of the denominations during the years immediately preceding and following the Civil War as a result of the influence of Charles G. Finney. They can best be understood, however, as a protest against what they regarded as the growing "worldliness" of the more conventional churches. In 1866 a writer in the Methodist *Christian Advocate* noted with satisfaction that "by virtue of the habits which religion inculcates and cherishes, our church members have as a body risen in the social scale, and thus become socially removed from the great body out of which most of them originally gathered." While he regarded this development as "natural" and "not undesirable," it did leave the less privileged with a feeling that they had been effectively disinherited religiously. Thus the Holiness churches from the beginning were "people's" churches, filling the void left when the older denominations became "middle class" and respectable or "worldly."

The Fundamentalist group is the most difficult of all to delimit. One reason for this difficulty is the fact that there were many "fundamentalist" churches embraced within the old-line denominations, and the co-operative activities of the Fundamentalist movement derived much of their support from members of conventional Baptist, Congregationalist, Methodist, Presbyterian, Quaker, and even Mennonite churches. The numerical total assigned to the Fundamentalist denominations, therefore, does not represent the full strength of the Fundamentalist movement. A second reason for the difficulty in delimiting the Fundamentalist group is that, while Fundamentalism in general represented a reaction against Modernism, some phases of the reaction were more culturally oriented and others theologically oriented. The Fundamentalist left wing represented by the Churches of Christ and dissident Baptist bodies, perhaps can best be understood as a protest against a culturally respectable urban middle-class Protestantism. The right wing, composed of the Orthodox Presbyterian Church and the Christian Reformed Church, was much more theologically oriented. Somewhere in the middle would be the Free Methodists and the Wesleyan Methodists who, during the course of the twentieth century, became characterized by a stronger emphasis upon the "fundamentals" than upon the Wesleyan concept of "holiness" or "sanctification." Finally, it is difficult to embrace all Fundamentalists within a single grouping because the movement was notably divisive, and some groups would not have wished to be classified with the others.

There were other Protestant bodies, not included in the Fundamentalist total, which also represented a "conservative" Protestantism that was out of sympathy with tendencies exhibited by most of the old-line churches. Neither the nine million Southern Baptists nor the two and one-half million Missouri and Wisconsin Synod Lutherans would wish to be classified as

American Protestantism

Fundamentalists, but they did represent in their diverse ways a "conservative" Protestantism equally unhappy to be identified with "cooperative Protestantism." Even greater theological affinities with Fundamentalism have been displayed by another six hundred thousand Protestants affiliated with such bodies as the various small Presbyterian churches, the Baptist General Conference of North America, the North American Baptist General Conference, the Evangelical Covenant Church, and the Salvation Army. Furthermore, the ten million members reportedly affiliated with the five large Negro Baptist and Methodist bodies would be difficult to distinguish theologically at many points from some of the Fundamentalist and Holiness groups.

The importance of this whole Adventist-Holiness-Fundamentalist-"conservative" wing of twentieth-century American Protestantism has frequently been minimized and obscured, but it embraces a vast grouping of more than thirty million adherents that represents to the popular mind much of the image of American Protestantism.

The shifting pattern of Protestant co-operation.—Another element in the changed configuration of American Protestantism in the twentieth century was the shift in the character of Protestant co-operation. Throughout the nineteenth century the voluntary societies had been the typical instruments of cooperative Protestant Action, and Fundamentalist groups continued to use the voluntary society pattern of co-operation effectively in the twentieth century. Youth for Christ, the Inter-Varsity Christian Fellowship, the Christian Business Men's Committee—all followed the earlier pattern. Even the National Association of Evangelicals, which linked some three or four million "fundamentalists" for purposes of co-operative action, was basically a voluntary society with membership available to individuals, local churches, and a variety of other organizations. But among the old-line denominations, this relatively spontaneous form of voluntary co-operation had largely been discarded.

This shift was brought about by the denominations themselves taking over many of the responsibilities formerly discharged through the interdenominational voluntary societies. The Christian Endeavor societies, for example, had been displaced in most of the churches by denominational "youth fellowships." The Student Christian Movement was largely replaced by denominational student groups. The Sunday school interest was diverted into denominational channels with denominational lesson materials being assiduously promoted. The Student Volunteer Movement continued to exist but only on the periphery of the denominations' efforts to recruit missionary personnel. The political and social concerns, which formerly had produced an array of independent societies each dedicated to a single objective, began to be expressed through official denominational boards of "social service" or "social action." Under these new conditions, what was needed was an "official" means of linking and co-ordinating these denominational activities.

After 1900 a cluster of official interdenominational agencies was formed for this specific purpose. Among these new agencies were the International Council of Religious Education, the Home Missions Council, the United Stewardship Council, and the Council of Church Women. By far the most important of these agencies, however, was the Federal Council of Churches, which was organized in 1908. Although the Federal Council as one of its objectives sought to foster a unified program of evangelism, its primary purpose was "to secure larger combined influence for the churches of Christ in all matters affecting the moral and social condition of the people, so as to promote the application of the law of Christ in every relation to human life," and the first act of the newly formed council was to draft a Social Creed of the Churches. Taken together, these various agencies, including the Foreign Missions Conference, which had been formed just prior to the beginning of the twentieth century, provided the means for co-ordinating every aspect of the work of the Protestant churches.

The distinguishing feature of these interdenominational bodies was their official character. Hitherto, interdenominational agencies had been voluntary agencies, maintained and supported by interested individuals. These new "councils" were quite different in that they were controlled directly by the participating denominations. The culmination of this movement was reached in 1950, when these various official agencies were brought together to form the National Council of Churches with divisions of Christian Education, Home Missions, Foreign Missions, and Christian Life and Work, and departments of Evangelism, Broadcasting and Films, Church World Service, United Church Men, and United Church Women.

While the national structure of "co-operative Protestantism" was taking shape, it was paralleled on the state and local level by the formation of state and city councils or federations of churches. In addition to implementing the general concerns which found expression at the national level, the local councils carried on a number of specific activities—joint programs of weekday religious education, teacher-training institutes, union services, hospital chaplaincies, youth programs, and comity arrangements.

Patterns of continuing growth and the problem of self-defini-

tion.—A study of the rate of growth of the various Protestant denominations between 1940 and 1954 suggests that numerically the old-line denominations of the nineteenth-century Protestant coalition are to be decreasingly prominent in the total configuration of American Protestant life. While there were a few individual exceptions, the denominations of "co-operative Protestantism" as a whole were not keeping pace in their growth with the increase of the population. The Presbyterians, Episcopalians, and United Lutherans were increasing proportionately somewhat more rapidly than the general population, but their gains were more than offset by the slower rate of growth of the other denominations of co-operative Protestantism.

The "growing edge" of Protestantism would seem to lie outside the circle of "co-operative Protestantism." The two major bodies that had striking records of growth during the 1940–54 period were the Southern Baptist Convention and the Lutheran Church–Missouri Synod, neither of which belonged to the National Council of Churches. From 1940 to 1954, the Southern Baptists increased from 4,949,174 to 8,163,562, a gain of 64.9 per cent in comparison with a population increase of 24 per cent. The Missouri Synod Lutherans during the same period increased from 1,298,798 to 1,932,000, for a gain of 48.9 per cent. Among the smaller "non–co-operative" bodies with records of conspicuous growth were the Christian Reformed Church with a gain of 61.6 per cent, the Church of God (Anderson, Ind.) with 59.3 per cent, the Church of the Nazarene with 57.4 per cent, and the Seventh-day Adventists with 53.2 per cent. The record of many of the smaller groups is very spotty and characterized by rapid gains and losses, but it is evident that these groups with their diverse characteristics have become a significant feature of twentieth-century Protestantism.

Protestantism's loss of identity was interpreted in the preceding chapter as primarily the product of the major old-line denominations having been transformed, through a process of assimilation, into institutional expressions of a culture religion which reflected rather than molded its culture. The present chapter has indicated how Protestantism, as a consequence, was increasingly fragmented by the impact of differing aspects of the culture. This loss of homogeneity and cohesiveness made much more difficult the task of self-definition which is indispensable to the recovery of Protestantism as a significant force in American life.

· 11 ·

PROSPECTS FOR RECOVERY

This picture of mid-twentieth-century American Protestantism may be unduly bleak. There were, of course, survivals among Protestants of earlier theological structures, although the survival of anything resembling classical Protestantism was isolated and meager. Furthermore, true faith and true piety continued to find expression in the lives of many individual members of the churches, for men and women can be found by Christ even in the midst of a situation in which he is misinterpreted and the gospel itself is obscured. Nevertheless, having said this, one finds little reason to question the validity of Alfred North Whitehead's judgment of Protestantism in 1933: "its dogmas no longer dominate; its divisions no longer interest; its institutions no longer direct the patterns of life." On the other hand, at the very time Whitehead pronounced this verdict, there were signs which pointed to a possible Protestant recovery. But before attention is directed to the prospect for a renewal of Protestant life and witness, Protestantism's loss of identity must be recalled and its plight briefly considered.

The plight of American Protestantism.—The popular image of the emptiness and formlessness of Protestantism was clearly revealed in the campaign which preceded the election of John F. Kennedy to the Presidency. When it was announced that Senator Kennedy, a Roman Catholic, would enter the West Virginia presidential primary, the political pundits immediately observed that, since 95 per cent of the people of West Virginia were Protestants, this primary would provide a thorough test of the bearing of the religious issue upon Senator Kennedy's availability as a potential nominee of the Democratic party. It is the 95 per cent Protestant figure that is of interest, for it was derived from the fact that slightly less than 5 per cent of the population of West Virginia was Roman Catholic. Actually only about 27 per cent of the people of West Virginia belonged to Protestant churches, but Protestantism was so devoid of definition and identity in the popular mind that it was assumed that everyone who was not Roman Catholic was automatically Protestant. The armed services of the United States had long operated on this same assumption, with the identification tags of all who were not Roman Catholics or Jews being stamped with a "P" to indicate that they were Protestants.

The prevalance of this assumption is not difficult to understand. It represents in part a lingering heritage from an earlier Protestant America when the whole culture was so thoroughly Protestant in orientation that it could be assumed that almost everyone who was not explicitly something else could be regarded as Protestant in background and unconscious conviction if not in specific affiliation. It represents, in the second place, the confused image of a Protestantism which had lost much of its unity and cohesiveness and had become diverse and multiform in its expression. Even Protestants, in the absence of any sense of a normative tradition, found it difficult to define and identify the Protestant community. The National Council of Churches reflected this confusion in its most extreme form when it listed the non-theist Ethical Culture Society and the Hindu Vedanta Society in the *Yearbook of the American Churches* among the Protestant denominations. Finally, many of the old-line Protestant churches did much to foster the popular impression that Protestantism represented nothing in particular and everything in general by quite frankly rejoicing in the loss of Protestant identity as evidence of an "ecumenical" spirit. They further obscured the borders of the Protestant community by allowing the earlier gathered churches to become community churches which made few demands and extended an indiscriminate welcome to all members of the community into their "fellowship."

Not only had Protestantism become difficult to define and to identify theologically; it had lost almost all forms of institutional expression which might have given at least an organizational identity to the Protestant community. One observer at a Memorial Day parade was somewhat puzzled by the round of applause which greeted two contingents as they marched by in contrast to the silence in which the rest of the parade was viewed, until he was informed that the applause had been evoked by units of the Catholic War Veterans and the Jewish War Veterans. The Protestant war veterans were lost in the generality of the community. What was true of the war veterans was true of almost all aspects of community life. There were Catholic welfare agencies and Jewish welfare agencies, but the former Protestant agencies had almost universally become community agencies. There were Catholic youth organizations and

Jewish youth organizations, but the Y.M.C.A. and the Y.W.C.A. which once had been the instruments of the Protestant churches had ceased to think of themselves as Protestant organizations.

To the extent that these formerly Protestant institutions were transformed into community agencies, the institutional symbols which might have conveyed a sense of organizational identity to the Protestant community not only were eliminated, but the possibility of any concerted Protestant Action was also ruled out. Throughout the nineteenth century, the common convictions of Protestants had been voiced and applied through a closely knit complex of voluntary societies. After 1900 these had been replaced by a cluster of official "councils" which, in turn, have been brought together to form the National Council of Churches.

Whatever its virtues, the National Council of Churches was not equipped to serve as either the voice or the arm of a united Protestantism. One reason for its inadequacy in this respect was the fact that Protestantism was far from united. The homogeneity of Protestantism in the successive Puritan, Puritan-Evangelical, and Methodist eras had long since disappeared. Furthermore, the National Council of Churches represented no more than a bare majority of the Protestant population, and its influence was also emasculated by the fact that it was weakest in those areas of the country where Protestantism was strongest.

The major reason for the inability of the National Council of Churches to serve as the voice and arm of Protestantism, however, was due to the fact that it did not conceive of itself as a Protestant instrument. With the fading of a Protestant consciousness, various non-Protestant bodies—the Armenian Church of North America, the Polish National Catholic Church, and the Greek, Rumanian, Russian, Serbian, Syrian, and Ukrainian Orthodox churches—had become members of the National Council of Churches. While this broadened participation had many values and presented at least the possibility of a fruitful "ecumenical" encounter, it made it impossible for the Council to speak and to act clearly and incisively in terms of Protestant interests and it effectively deprived the Protestant community of its one surviving institutionalized symbol.

The transformation of the National Council of Churches into a non-Protestant body—a process which began with the earlier Federal Council of Churches—can only be regarded as reflecting the prevailing opinion of its constituent Protestant bodies that it was not important for the Protestant community to have an instrument of Protestant action through which it could voice and apply its common convictions. Such a need could be viewed with relative indifference presumably because the denominations themselves, to say nothing of the Protestant community as a whole, were not conscious of possessing many common convictions. Most of the denominations embraced within themselves such disparate views that the possibility of any extensive denominational consensus was ruled out.

Even the pronouncements which the clergy found it possible to agree upon from time to time in their denominational assemblies frequently carried little weight because they did not represent the consensus of denominational opinion, lay opinion being sharply divergent from that of the clergy. In the absence of criteria provided by a normative tradition and with the disappearance of disciplinary procedures, the plight of many Protestant churches was illustrated in exaggerated form by an incident which is reported to have occurred in a Baptist assembly. The speaker had been enumerating what Baptists believe and when he asked for discussion from the floor, a man rose to his feet and said, "I don't believe any of those things, and I am a Baptist." Whereupon the speaker responded, "You don't have to believe them to be a Baptist." Operating within such a context, it is scarcely surprising that the constituent denominations of the National Council of Churches had little reason to believe that their Protestant witness would be made less incisive by subordinating it—in the pronouncements of the National Council—to a consensus that took into account the views of non-Protestant churches.

The theological revival.—In the midst of their several surrenders, the denominations of American Protestantism still carried within themselves—in the form of surviving memories and a lingering identification with the resources of historic Christianity—the possibility of a recovery of a clearer sense of their vocation as Christian churches. For in these surviving memories, however much their normative theology might be eroded and their Christianity identified with current forms of the American way of life, there was available to them a reminder of the summons of a jealous God calling upon them to worship and serve him alone.

One of the major obstacles to a Protestant recovery during the first three decades of the twentieth century was the fact that theological issues had become involved in the highly emotional partisan debate engendered by the Modernist-Fundamentalist controversy. The effect of this controversy was to force both camps into more and more extreme and untenable positions, to inhibit calm and careful consideration of the issues at stake, and to cause many to regard all theological discussion with apprehension and even distaste. By 1930, however, it was apparent that the attempt to place the major denominations in the ill-considered strait jacket of Fundamentalism was not going to be successful. With this immediate threat removed and sobered by the depression years, some of the leaders of the churches were in a mood to be more receptive to what had been a major contention of Fundamentalism at its best. At its best, Fundamentalism had held out for a faith that was something more than insights derived from the contemporary culture. The most conspicuous illustration of the change that took place was Harry Emerson Fosdick's confession in 1935 that "the church must go beyond modernism."

We have been all things to all men long enough. We have adapted and adjusted and accommodated and conceded long enough. We have at times gotten so low down that we talked as though the highest compliment that could be paid to Almighty God was that a few scientists believed in him. Yet all the time, by right, we had an independent standing-ground and a message of our own in which alone there is hope for mankind.

The church, he insisted, must cease seeking to accommodate itself to the prevailing culture and must stand out from it and challenge it, for the "unescapable fact," which has been testified to again and again in Christian history, is the fact that Christ cannot be "harmonized" with any culture. What Christ does to culture is to "challenge" it.

The beginning of this change in climate had been signaled by Henry Nelson Wieman's announcement in 1932 of his intention "to promote a theocentric religion as over against the prevalent anthropocentric one," although it was left to others to grasp the full meaning of the sickness into which American Protestantism had fallen. Much more significant as initial landmarks in Protestantism's attempt to recover an independent perspective was the publication in that same year of Reinhold Niebuhr's

Moral Man and Immoral Society and the arrival of Paul Tillich the following year to teach at Union Theological Seminary, for these two men in their diverse ways symbolized the role that European theological and philosophical thinking was to play in the reconstruction of American Protestantism. While there were only isolated voices calling for a theological recovery during that decade, in the 1940's a theological revival became increasingly evident in Protestant theological seminaries. During the years that followed, a growing segment of the clergy was caught up in the theological renaissance, but it still remained an open question whether Protestantism was to recover its full vigor. To do so, its theological structure needed to be further clarified, the new theological interest needed to penetrate the laity, and Protestant church life needed to undergo reform and reconstruction in terms of the developing understanding of the Christian faith.

The future?—The recovery of American Protestantism as a Christian tradition, with sufficient integrity and independence of perspective to enable it to meet the challenge of the world and the challenge of other religious traditions with a sharp challenge of its own, will not come full blown from the Protestant community as a whole. It will arise from within segments of the Protestant community and a price will have to be paid for the recovery. The United Church of Christ, making a fresh beginning, voiced the conviction that one of the greatest needs is the need for "integrity of church membership," but this will be difficult to achieve in a success-minded era when immediate numbers are prized more highly than depth of commitment, even though it has been demonstrated that lack of commitment —in the long run—results in declining numbers. From what quarter, then, is the recovery most likely to come?

What Henry Pitt VanDusen described as "third force" Protestantism—the miscellaneous threefold grouping of Adventist, Fundamentalist, and Holiness churches—has exhibited both vigor and vitality during the middle decades of the twentieth century, and it has several assets which may enable it to blaze the way to a Protestant recovery. These groups at least possess the virtue of talking about something definite and specific. Furthermore, however partial and inadequate it may be, they have some sense of continuity with historic Christianity, as well as doctrinal criteria for self-definition and self-identity. Moreover, they have displayed a ready willingness to refuse to conform to many dominant cultural pressures.

The "third force," on the other hand, has been unduly obscurantist and legalistic, often exhibiting a willingness to bypass thinking entirely and frequently dissipating its strength in unnecessarily bitter and divisive sectarian struggles and conflicts. Much of its otherwise admirable intransigence, furthermore, seems to be rooted in a recalcitrant resistance to the modern world that finds much of its motivation in a parochial view of the Christian faith that is no less culture-bound than the understanding of the Christian faith exemplified in many other churches. The possibility of a more creative response is suggested by the criticism at these points that has begun to be voiced from within the "third force" itself by those who have been variously described as "neo-Fundamentalists" or "neo-'Evangelicals'."

The Southern Baptists represent another "growing edge" of American Protestantism, but a large segment of Southern Baptist life displays many of the weaknesses of "third force" Protestantism. Southern Baptist self-criticism finds the secret of much of the Southern Baptist growth in a highly geared promotional program that is lacking in depth and capitalizes upon the emotions aroused by a regional self-consciousness. Such self-criticism reflects a developing theological sensitivity and concern, but in a denomination of almost ten million members it is not sufficiently widespread to suggest what the future contribution of Southern Baptists is to be. There is a similar uncertainty of the future for the American Baptists, the Methodists, the Disciples of Christ, and the major Negro denominations. While trends and characteristics vary among them, there are only a few clues to indicate that their church life may be redirected and reconstructed.

Of the other major old-line Protestant denominations, the Presbyterians and the Episcopalians have exhibited most evidence of continuing growth. This growth may be due to the fact that American Protestantism has become increasingly stratified socially during the twentieth century, with the result that the Presbyterians and Episcopalians have been able to profit in suburbia from the prestige that accrued to them as upper- and upper-middle-class denominations. The continued adherence of the Presbyterians to their traditional doctrinal symbols and the centering of the liturgical life of the Episcopalians in the Prayer Book also may have protected both denominations from the full corrosive effect of the "acids of modernity." Whatever the basis of their growth, both denominations—in their diverse ways, to be sure—have manifested a deepening interest in the theological revival and have initiated proposals to give greater form and substance to their church life. In this endeavor, they have been immeasurably aided by the fact that they could draw upon the resources of a tradition that had not been completely forgotten.

It is significant that the Evangelical and Reformed Church contributed the most notable initial leadership to the theological revival in the persons of the two Niebuhrs. As a result of its union with the Congregationalists in the new United Church of Christ, the Evangelical and Reformed Church has committed its future to the hope that the blending of two diverse traditions will accentuate the strengths represented by each of them. Perhaps the eager concern of both parties to the merger to transcend the cultural differences imbedded in their respective traditions will free them to pursue more vigorously the endeavor to become a more faithful church than either of them had been heretofore.

The final prospect for a vigorous renewal of Protestant life and witness rests with the Lutheran churches which had overcome much of their fragmentation by 1960 and had grouped themselves into three main bodies. All had exhibited an ability to grow during the post–World War II years, with the Lutheran Church–Missouri Synod making the greatest gains. The Lutheran churches are in the fortunate position of having been, in varying degrees, insulated from American life for a long period of time. As a result they have been less subject to the theological erosion which so largely stripped other denominations of an awareness of their continuity with a historic Christian tradition. Thus the resources of the Christian past have been more readily available to them, and this fact suggests that they may have an increasingly important role in a Protestant recovery. Among the assets immediately at hand among the Lutherans are a confessional tradition, a surviving liturgical structure, and a sense of community which, however much it may be the product of cultural factors, may make it easier for them than for most Protestant denominations to recover the "integrity of church membership" without which Protestants are ill-equipped to participate effectively in the dialogue of a pluralistic society.

Important Dates

1607	First Anglican worship in Virginia
1620	Separatist Congregationalists establish Plymouth colony
1626	First Dutch Reformed worship in New Netherlands
1630	Great migration of non-separatist Congregationalists to Massachusetts Bay begins
1636	Roger Williams banished from Massachusetts Bay and settles at Providence Thomas Hooker founds Connecticut Harvard College founded by Massachusetts Bay Congregationalists to provide an educated ministry
1639	First Baptist church organized by Roger Williams at Providence First Lutheran worship in New Sweden
1640	Long Parliament meets in England
1642–49	English civil wars

1643–49 Westminster Assembly

1648 Cambridge Synod and Platform

1649 George Fox begins his public ministry in England

1656 Quaker itinerants imprisoned at Boston

1657 Half-way Covenant adopted by Congregationalists

1660 Restoration of the Stuarts in England

1675 West Jersey becomes the first Quaker colony

1681 Pennsylvania founded by William Penn

1684 Massachusetts charter revoked

1688 Glorious Revolution in England

1689 Act of Toleration adopted by English Parliament
James Blair becomes first Commissary of the bishop of London in Virginia

1690 Mennonites establish separate worship

1693 College of William and Mary founded to train Anglican clergy

1701 Society for the Propagation of the Gospel founded

1706 Presbytery of Philadelphia formed

1707 Philadelphia Baptist Association formed
Yale College founded by Connecticut Congregationalists
Trial of Francis Makemie
English colonies become British with the establishment of the United Kingdom

1708 Connecticut Congregationalists adopt Saybrook Platform

Important Dates

1710   John Wise publishes *The Churches' Quarrel Espoused*

1723   First Dunker church organized

1725   First German Reformed church organized

1726   Beginning of Great Awakening in New Jersey under Frelinghuysen
William Tennent establishes "log college"

1729   Wesleys organize "holy club" at Oxford University
Presbyterian "Adopting Act" accepts Westminster Confession of Faith

1734   Jonathan Edwards and Great Awakening at Northampton

1735   Moravians settle in Georgia

1737   Quakers adopt "birthright" membership

1739   George Whitefield begins his American tours

1741–58   Old Side–New Side division among the Presbyterians

1742   Henry M. Muhlenberg arrives to assume leadership of German Lutherans

1746   Princeton established to provide Presbyterian ministers

1765   Brown University founded by Baptists

1779   Virginia Statute of Religious Liberty

1784   Methodist Church established at Christmas Conference in Baltimore

1789   General Convention of Protestant Episcopal Church organized
First meeting of Presbyterian General Assembly

1791   Adoption of First Amendment to United States Constitution

1793   Synod of the German Reformed Church organized

1794   James O'Kelly forms group in Virginia resolved to be known only as "Christians"

1800   First of the "camp meeting" revivals in the West

1801   Plan of Union adopted by Presbyterians and Congregationalists

1804   Barton W. Stone forms group in Kentucky resolved to be known only as "Christians"

1809   "Christian Association" formed by Thomas Campbell in Pennsylvania

1810   American Board of Commissioners for Foreign Missions

1814   General Convention of the Baptist Denomination organized

1815   Unitarian defection from Congregationalists in Massachusetts

1816   American Education Society
New York City Mission Society

1817   Congregationalism disestablished in New Hampshire

1818   Congregationalism disestablished in Connecticut

1820   General Synod of Evangelical (Lutheran) Church formed

1824   American Sunday School Union

1825   American Tract Society

1825–35   Finney revivals

1826   American Home Missionary Society

Important Dates

1829–31   The great "Valley Campaign" of the voluntary societies

1832   Followers of Barton W. Stone and Alexander Campbell coalesce as "Disciples" or "Christians"

1833   Congregationalism disestablished in Massachusetts

1837   New School Synods ejected by Presbyterian General Assembly and Plan of Union abrogated

1843–44   "Millerite" excitement occasioned by "end of age" expectation

1845   Methodist and Baptists divide over issue of slavery

1847   Lutheran Church–Missouri Synod constituted
Horace Bushnell publishes *Christian Nurture*

1851   Y.M.C.A. organized at Boston

1857   Christian Reformed secession from Dutch Reformed Church

1857–58   "Prayer meeting" revivals

1860   Augustana (Swedish) Lutheran Synod organized

1867   American branch of Evangelical Alliance formed

1869   American Sunday School Convention (International Sunday School Association, International Council of Religious Education)

1870–92   Dwight L. Moody revival campaigns

1872   Uniform Lessons adopted

1885   Young People's Society of Christian Endeavor

1886   Student Volunteer Movement

1889   Christian Socialist Society

1893   Foreign Missions Conference of North America

1907   Walter Rauschenbusch publishes *Christianity and the Social Crisis*

1908   Federal Council of Churches of Christ in America

1909–12 Publication of *The Fundamentals* in response to "modernist" tendencies

1919   World's Christian Fundamentals Association

1919–22 Interchurch World Movement

1932   Laymen's Missionary Inquiry
        Reinhold Niebuhr publishes *Moral Man and Immoral Society*

1939   Methodist Episcopal Church, Methodist Episcopal Church South, and Methodist Protestant Church unite to form the Methodist Church

1950   National Council of Churches formed by merging several interdenominational councils and agencies

1957   General Council of the Congregational Christian Churches and the General Synod of the Evangelical and Reformed Church merge to form the United Church of Christ

1960   Smaller Lutheran bodies form the Lutheran Church in America and the American Lutheran Church

Bibliographical Notes

CHAPTER I

Statistics on the national and ecclesiastical background of the colonial population are presented and discussed in Clinton Rossiter, *Seedtime of the Republic* (1953), pp. 150–51; C. D. Paullin, *Atlas of the Historical Geography of the United States* (1932), p. 50; and W. L. Sperry, *Religion in America* (1946), pp. 264–71.

Section 1, "Protestant Diversity": The Anglican view of other churches is discussed in Norman F. Sykes, *Old Priest and New Presbyter* (1956), pp. 7, 18–20; the significance of unlimited space is elaborated by S. E. Mead, "The American People: Their Space, Time, and Religion," *Journal of Religion*, XXXIV (1954), 244–55; and documentation for the discussion of the theological foundations of freedom is found in W. S. Hudson, *The Great Tradition of the American Churches* (1953).

Section 2, "The Common Heritage": The Calvinist heritage of the colonial churches is emphasized by Ralph Gabriel, *The Course of American Democratic Thought* (1940); the John Witherspoon quotation is from *Essays on Important Subjects* (1805), IV, 203; a full discussion of the role of the laity, from which several quotations have been taken, is given by S. E. Mead, "The Rise of the Evangelical Conception of the Ministry" in H. R. Niebuhr (ed.), *The Ministry in Historical Perspectives* (1956); and the nineteenth century as the Methodist age in America is the verdict of R. E. Thompson, *A History of the Presbyterian Churches in the United States* (1895), p. 34, and L. W. Bacon, *A History of American Christianity* (1897), p. 176.

Section 3, "The Concept of Denominationalism": The Wesley quotation is from "The Character of a Methodist," Wesley's *Works* (1841), VIII, 332–33; Luther's views are given in Wilhelm Pauck, *The Heritage of the Reformation* (1950), p. 33; the case for denominationalism, as developed by the Dissenting Brethren, is discussed and documented in W. S. Hudson, "Denominationalism as a Basis for Ecumenicity," *Church History*, XXIV (1955), 37–47; the Davies and Tennent quotations are found in Samuel Davies, *Sermons on Important Subjects* (1842), I, 217–18, and L. J. Trinterud, *The Forming of an American Tradition* (1949), p. 132.

CHAPTER II

Section 4, "The Churches in the Post-Revolutionary Era": The pessimistic views of Anglican prospects are cited by L. W. Bacon, *A History of American Christianity* (1897), pp. 213, 232, and of Methodism by J. M. Buckley, *A History of Methodists in the United States* (1896), p. 186; the Bushnell quotations in this and the two following sections are from *Barbarism, the First Danger* (1847).

Section 5, "The Task of the Churches Defined": The quotations illustrating the views of the Massachusetts Bay leaders are drawn from Perry Miller, *The New England Mind: The Seventeenth Century* (1939), pp. 398–431; the alliance of rationalists and pietists is described by S. E. Mead, "American Protestantism during the Revolutionary Epoch," *Church History*, XXII (1953), 278–97; Timothy Dwight's views on the utility of western migration are cited by A. F. Tyler, *Freedom's Ferment* (1944).

Section 6, "The Protestant Counter-offensive": The role of the voluntary societies is the theme of C. F. Foster, *An Errand of Mercy: The Evangelical United Front, 1790–1837* (1960); the opposition to an educated ministry is discussed by W. W. Sweet, *Religion on the American Frontier* (1931–39), I, 68–74; estimates of the ratio of church membership in 1800, 1835, and 1850 are given by C. C. Cole, *The Social Ideals of the Northern Evangelists, 1826–1860* (1954), pp. 13–14.

Section 7, "The Realignment of American Protestantism": The

membership statistics are given in W. W. Sweet, *The American Churches: An Interpretation* (1947), p. 42; the characterization of Methodism is based on S. E. Mead, "Professor Sweet's Religion in America," *Church History*, XXII (1953), 42–44, and "American Protestantism during the Revolutionary Epoch," *ibid*, pp. 290–92.

Section 8, "A Protestant America": The initial summary of Protestant dominance is based on R. T. Handy, "The Protestant Quest for a Christian America, 1830–1930," *Church History*, XXII (1953), 10–12.

CHAPTER III

The views of Theodore Roosevelt are reported by C. A. and M. R. Beard, *The Rise of American Civilization* (1927), II, 399–400, and H. G. McMahon, *Chautauqua County: A History* (1958), p. 221; for the analysis of revivalism, see S. E. Mead, "Denominationalism: The Shape of American Protestantism," *Church History*, XXIII (1954), 307–10.

Section 9, "Protestantism's Loss of Identity": The New Theology and its more conspicuous exponents are discussed in W. S. Hudson, *The Great Tradition of the American Churches* (1953); the distinction between constructive and radical Fundamentalism is made by Norman H. Maring in "Conservative but Progressive," *What Hath God Wrought*, ed. G. L. Guffin (1960), pp. 17–28; the statement that "schism is the normal state of the church" is from L. W. Bacon, *A History of American Christianity*, p. 309.

Section 10, "The New Configuration of American Protestantism": The statistics are from the *Yearbook of the American Churches for 1960* (1959) which gives the Protestant total as 61,504,699. This figure is inflated by including many who are non-Protestant in the sense that they neither consider themselves Protestants nor look to the Reformation as a decisive recovery and restatement of the Christian faith. With regard to the statistical tabulation: the Baptist total is restricted to those bodies which participate in the Baptist World Alliance; the Methodist total includes the Evangelical United Brethren Church but not the Free Methodist or Wesleyan Methodist Church; the Fundamentalist total combines denominations which exhibit some diverse tendencies with the Churches of Christ and dissident Baptist groups representing the left wing and the Christian Reformed Church the right wing; the major holiness groups are Assemblies of God, Church of God in Christ, and Church of the Nazarene; the statistics of the Congregationalists and the Evangelical and Reformed Churches continue to be reported separately pending the completion of their merger.

Section 11, "Prospects for Recovery": Protestant denominations affiliated with the National Council of Churches reported a total membership in 1958 of some thirty-six million. It must be remembered, however, that there was strong opposition to the National Council in almost all the constituent Protestant bodies. Furthermore, ten million of the thirty-six million total was represented by the claimed membership of five Negro bodies. This claimed membership is obviously greatly inflated, for the total claimed Negro membership exceeds the total Negro population over thirteen years of age.

Suggested Reading

GENERAL WORKS

The most widely used general history of American Protestantism has been W. E. Sweet, *The Story of Religion in America* (rev. ed., 1950), which is basically an account of institutional developments. Some of Sweet's themes were first developed by H. K. Rowe, *The History of Religion in the United States* (1924). A perceptive critique of Sweet's assumptions is given by S. E. Mead, "Professor Sweet's 'Religion and Culture in America,'" *Church History,* XXII (1953), 33–49. Texts of important source materials are provided by R. T. Handy, L. A. Loetscher, and H. Shelton Smith, *American Christianity: An Historical Interpretation with Representative Documents* (1960). There are many handbooks which describe the distinctive tenets of the various Protestant groups, but the best informed and most useful of these is F. E. Mayer, *The Religious Bodies of America* (2d ed., 1956). The most convenient source of Protestant statistics is the *Yearbook of the American Churches,* published annually by the National Council of Churches. E. S. Gaustad, *Historical Atlas of American Religion* (1961) is a useful reference tool.

Many attempts have been made to characterize American Protestantism. One of the earliest and most successful attempts was Robert Baird, *Religion in America* (1856). Almost a century later,

American Protestantism

W. L. Sperry produced an informative essay under the same title, *Religion in America* (1946), to interpret American Protestantism to British readers. R. E. Osborn, *The Spirit of American Protestantism* (1958) is a relatively enthusiastic appraisal of the same genre. A more sober and critical analysis has been provided by M. E. Marty, *The New Shape of American Religion* (1959).

The most influential discussion of the dominant theological motifs in American Protestantism has been H. Richard Neibuhr, *The Kingdom of God in America* (1937). W. S. Hudson, *The Great Tradition of the American Churches* (1953) relates these theological developments to the institutional life of the churches. Wilhelm Pauck, "Theology in the Life of Contemporary American Protestantism," *Shane Quarterly*, XIII (1952), 37–50, is a highly perceptive account of the factors that contributed to the non-theological character of much of American Protestantism. The most stimulating and suggestive discussion of the basic character of American Protestantism, however, is to be found in a series of essays by S. E. Mead, "From Coercion to Persuasion: Another Look at the Rise of Religious Liberty and the Emergence of Denominationalism," *Church History*, XXV (1956), 317–37; "Denominationalism: The Shape of Protestantism in America," *ibid.*, XXIII (1954), 291–320; "American Protestantism since the Civil War," *Journal of Religion*, XXXVI (1956), 1–16, 67–89. Mead's interpretative pattern is further elaborated in "American Protestantism during the Revolutionary Epoch," *Church History*, XXII (1953), 279–97; "The American People: Their Space, Time, and Religion," *Journal of Religion*, XXXIV (1954), 244–55; "Abraham Lincoln's 'Last, Best Hope of Earth': The American Dream of Destiny and Democracy," *Church History*, XXIII (1954), 3–16; and "The Rise of the Evangelical Conceptions of the Ministry in America, 1607–1850," in *The Ministry in Historical Perspectives*, ed. H. R. Niebuhr and D. D. Williams (1956).

The impact of American Protestantism upon American society is discussed by E. S. Bates, *American Faith* (1940), R. H. Gabriel, *The Course of American Democratic Thought* (1940), and A. F. Tyler, *Freedom's Ferment* (1944).

DENOMINATIONAL HISTORIES

The "American Church History Series," published initially in the 1890's by the Christian Literature Company and subsequently

Suggested Reading

by Charles Scribner's Sons, provides separate volumes for the major Protestant denominations. Among more recent denominational studies are: R. G. Torbet, *History of the Baptists* (1950); W. S. Hudson (ed.), *Baptist Concepts of the Church* (1959); G. G. Atkins and F. L. Fagley, *History of American Congregationalism* (1942); W. E. Garrison and A. T. DeGroot, *The Disciples of Christ* (1948); W. W. Manross, *History of the American Episcopal Church* (rev. ed., 1950); A. R. Wentz, *A Basic History of Lutheranism in America* (1955); H. E. Luccock, Paul Hutchinson, and R. W. Goodloe, *The Story of Methodism* (1949); G. J. Slosser (ed.), *They Seek a Country: The American Presbyterians* (1955); and L. A. Loetscher, *The Broadening Church: A Study of Theological Issues in the Presbyterian Church since 1865* (1954).

W. W. Sweet, *Religion in Colonial America* (1942) is a standard account. Perry Miller has been responsible for a major reinterpretation of New England Puritanism as a result of his several volumes, most notably, *Orthodoxy in Massachusetts, 1630–1650* (1933); *The New England Mind: The Seventeenth Century* (1939); and *The New England Mind: From Colony to Province* (1953). L. J. Trinterud, *The Forming of an American Tradition* (1949) is an important reassessment of colonial Presbyterianism. The Great Awakening has been treated in a series of volumes: E. S. Gaustad, *The Great Awakening in New England* (1957); C. H. Maxson, *The Great Awakening in the Middle Colonies* (1920); and W. M. Gewehr, *The Great Awakening in Virginia* (1930). A. P. Stokes, *Church and State in the United States* (1950) and J. H. Nichols, *Democracy and the Churches* (1951) both discuss the development of religious liberty.

PRE–CIVIL WAR AMERICA

W. W. Sweet, *Religion in the Development of American Culture, 1765–1840* (1952) deals with various facets of Protestant life during this period. He has also devoted several volumes to *Religion on the American Frontier:* Vol. I, *The Baptists* (1931); Vol. II, *The Presbyterians* (1936); Vol. III, *The Congregationalists* (1939); Vol. IV, *The Methodists* (1946). Two comprehensive studies of revivalism are: W. G. McLoughlin, *Modern Revivalism* (1959) and B. A. Weisberger, *They Gathered at the River* (1958). Of related interest are: C. A. Johnson, *The Frontier Camp Meeting* (1955) and W. R. Cross, *The Burned-over District: The Social and Intellectual History of Enthusiastic Religion in Western New York, 1800–1850* (1950). The latter volume is of major importance as a case study of the transmission of New England culture.

The rise of the voluntary societies as an expression of Protestant social concern is detailed by C. I. Foster, *An Errand of Mercy: The Evangelical United Front, 1790–1837* (1960). Different facets of the same concern are discussed by J. R. Bodo, *The Protestant Clergy and Public Issues, 1817–1848* (1954); C. C. Cole, *The Social Ideas of the Northern Evangelists, 1826–1860* (1954); and T. L. Smith, *Revivalism and Social Reform in Mid-Nineteenth Century America* (1957). More specialized studies of this same interest are: O. W. Elsbree, *Rise of the Missionary Spirit in America, 1790–1815* (1928); C. B. Goodykoontz, *Home Missions on the American Frontier* (1939); and D. G. Tewksbury, *The Founding of American Colleges and Universities before the Civil War* (1932).

POST–CIVIL WAR AMERICA

The post–Civil War period is covered by several of the general works previously mentioned, and they may be supplemented by two relatively popular surveys: W. E. Garrison, *The March of Faith* (1933); and G. G. Atkins, *Religion in Our Time* (1932). An important essay which has given direction to much research in this period is A. M. Schlesinger, "A Critical Period in American Protestantism, 1875–1900," *Massachusetts Historical Society Proceedings*, LXIV (1930). The author suggested that Protestantism faced two great challenges during the last quarter of the nineteenth century—the one to its system of thought, the other to its social program.

The latter problem has received major attention from C. H. Hopkins, *The Rise of the Social Gospel* (1940); A. I. Abell, *The Urban Impact on American Protestantism* (1943); and H. F. May, *Protestant Churches and Industrial America* (1949). Critical appraisals of the "social gospel" have been made by W. A. Visser t'Hooft, *The Background of the Social Gospel in America* (1928); and G. Hammar, *Christian Realism in Contemporary American Theology* (1940). The response of Protestants to one particular facet of the challenge to its system of thought has been delineated

Suggested Reading

by R. Hofstadter, *Social Darwinism in American Thought* (1945).

An early phase of the movement toward unity among Protestants has been depicted by C. H. Hopkins, *History of the Y.M.C.A. in North America* (1951). The major twentieth-century movement has been described by J. A. Hutchison, *We Are Not Divided: A Critical and Historical Study of the Federal Council of Churches* (1941); and an account of the formation of the National Association of Evangelicals has been provided by J. D. Murch, *Cooperation without Compromise* (1956).

A. S. Nash (ed.), *Protestant Thought in the Twentieth Century* (1951) is a very convenient and useful summary of developments in the several fields of theological study during the first half of the twentieth century. N. F. Furniss, *The Fundamentalist Controversy, 1918–1931* (1954) details the outward facts, but it should be balanced by J. G. Machen's statement of the Fundamentalist position, *Christianity and Liberalism* (1930). *Re-thinking Missions: A Laymen's Inquiry* (1932) is an important document reflecting the theological climate of the time, and related to it is the perceptive essay of R. T. Handy, "The American Religious Depression, 1925–1953," *Church History*, XXIX (1960), 3–16. The continuing social interest is discussed by R. M. Miller, *American Protestantism and Social Issues* (1958), and P. A. Carter, *The Decline and Revival of the Social Gospel, 1920–1940* (1956).

Acknowledgments

Perhaps the greatest pleasure of writing even a small book is that it calls to mind a long list of friends who have been one's benefactors. Even a monograph of brief compass cannot escape dependence upon others, but an essay that deals with many different groups over a period of more than three centuries can seldom claim to be wholly the product of independent research. This book is no exception. Its debts are many and varied. While some of the material and interpretations are the product of my own investigations and reflection, much has been borrowed from others.

The suggested readings and the bibliographical notes indicate most of my debts, but they scarcely reveal the extent of the contribution that has been made by a close circle of friends—most notably by Sidney E. Mead, whose insights have been fresh and illuminating; Robert T. Handy, whose judgments have been balanced and judicious; Leonard J. Trinterud, whose counsel has always been to the point; and James H. Nichols, whose careful reading of the manuscript has contributed greatly to whatever value the book may have. Furthermore, the editor, Professor Daniel J. Boorstin, subjected the manuscript to more helpful and detailed criticism than anyone could have any right to expect. To him I owe heartfelt gratitude.

Quite unavoidably, I have drawn upon my other writings, among

Acknowledgments

them: *The Great Tradition of the American Churches* (New York: Harper & Bros., 1953); a series of studies of "American Protestantism" in *Crossroads*, April–June, 1957, published by the Presbyterian Church, U.S.A.; and an essay on "Protestantism in Post-Protestant America" in *The Roman Catholic Church and the American Way of Life*, ed. T. T. McAvoy (South Bend, Ind., University of Notre Dame Press, 1960).

No author finishes a manuscript without being fully aware of its inadequacies and without being tempted to delay publication pending further study and reflection. In this situation, it is somewhat reassuring to recall John Dury's paraphrase of the words of Koheleth in Ecclesiastes: "If one observes the wind too narrowly, he will never sow his seed."

Index

Index

Index

Index

70–74, 86, 89, 91 f., 95, 97–101, 107, 109, 116, 125–28, 151, 156, 160 f., 175
Michaelius, Jonas, 25
Miller, Francis P., 135
Miller, Perry, 26
Millerites, 107
Mills, Samuel J., 85
Mississippi Valley, 85
Modernism, 146 f., 161
Modernist-Fundamentalist controversy, 143–49, 154, 171 f.
Moody, Dwight L., 112, 114, 118 f., 123
Moravians, 4, 18, 51
Mormonism, 107
Muhlenberg, Henry, 22, 26
Murray, John, 105

Nash, Arnold S., 129
National Association of Evangelicals, 162
National Council of Churches, 158, 164, 165, 168–71
Negro denominations, 175, 186
New Amsterdam, 6 f., 25
New Brunswick Presbytery, 31
New Divinity, 102, 105, 108
New England, 10 ff., 16, 20 f., 25–29, 31 f., 52, 61 f., 68–71, 80, 85, 90, 92, 98, 102 f.
New Hampshire, 22, 31, 52, 53
New Jersey, 6, 21 ff., 31, 56
New Lights and Old Lights, 31 f.
New Orleans, 126
New School–Old School division, 53, 105–9
New Sides and Old Sides, 31 f., 53
New Theology, 137–44, 149, 154
New York, 6, 52, 55, 92, 101
New York City, 142 f.
Niebuhr, H. Richard, 148, 175
Niebuhr, Reinhold, 172 f., 175
North Carolina, 56
Nova Scotia, 21

Oberlin College, 102
Ohio, 85, 88, 95
O'Kelley, James, 59

Orthodox Presbyterian Church, 161

Parish system, 27 ff., 78
Parker, Daniel, 93
Parkhurst, Charles A., 125
Peck, John Mason, 87 ff.
Penn, William, 6, 62
Pennsylvania, 6, 21 f., 52, 56, 59, 62
Pennsylvania, University of, 60
Pentecostal groups, 160
Philadelphia Baptist Association, 21, 53, 60
Philadelphia Sunday and Adult School Union, 83
Plan of Union, 24, 52, 108
Plymouth, 5, 20
Polish National Catholic Church, 69
Presbyterians, 4, 14–18, 20–24, 27, 31 ff., 42, 51–54, 60, 86, 89, 93 ff., 97 f., 101–8, 116, 151, 156, 161, 165, 175
Presbytery of Philadelphia, 21
Princeton University, 24, 60 f.
Protestant Action, 78, 84, 133, 162, 170
Protestant coalition, 59–62, 78, 81, 90, 92, 97, 105–9
Protestant dominance, 4, 109 ff., 124–28, 130–33, 140, 167
Protestant unity, 17–33, 40–48, 69 f., 83, 86, 111, 153 f., 162 f., 167 f.
Provost, Bishop, 57
Puritan Revolution, 8, 14, 20, 37, 40

Quakers (Society of Friends), 4, 6, 12, 22, 51, 55, 156, 161

Reformed Church in America, see Dutch Reformed
Restoration of 1660, 8, 20, 44
Revivalism, 78–81, 85, 101–4, 110, 114, 118 f., 122
Revivals of 1857–59, 102, 110, 114
Rhode Island, 12, 21, 52, 60
Robinson, John, 11
Roman Catholics, 4, 6, 8, 126, 129 ff., 153, 167 f.
Roosevelt, Theodore, 92 f., 128

Index